Powerarchy

Powerarchy

Understanding the Psychology of Oppression for Social Transformation

MELANIE JOY, PhD

BK°

Berrett–Koehler Publishers, Inc.

Berrett-Koehler Publishers, Inc.
1333 Broadway, Suite 1000
Oakland, CA 94612–1921
Tel: (510) 817–2277   Fax: (510) 817–2278 www.bkconnection.com

Ordering Information
Quantity sales. Special discounts are available on quantity purchases by corporations, associations, and others. For details, contact the "Special Sales Department" at the Berrett-Koehler address above.
Individual sales. Berrett-Koehler publications are available through most bookstores. They can also be ordered directly from Berrett-Koehler: Tel: (800) 929–2929; Fax: (802) 864–7626; www.bkconnection.com
Orders for college textbook/course adoption use. Please contact Berrett-Koehler: Tel: (800) 929–2929; Fax: (802) 864–7626.

Distributed to the U.S. trade and internationally by Penguin Random House Publisher Services.

Berrett-Koehler and the BK logo are registered trademarks of Berrett-Koehler Publishers, Inc.
Printed in the United States of America

Berrett-Koehler books are printed on long-lasting acid-free paper. When it is available, we choose paper that has been manufactured by environmentally responsible processes. These may include using trees grown in sustainable forests, incorporating recycled paper, minimizing chlorine in bleaching, or recycling the energy produced at the paper mill.

Library of Congress Cataloging-in-Publication Data
Names: Joy, Melanie, author.
Title: Powerarchy : understanding the psychology of oppression
    for social transformation / Melanie Joy.
Description: First Edition. | Oakland, CA : Berrett-Koehler Publishers, 2019.
Identifiers: LCCN 2019007344 | ISBN 9781523086665 (hardback)
Subjects: LCSH: Authority. | Control (Psychology) | Political psychology. | Power (Social
    sciences) | BISAC: PSYCHOLOGY / Social Psychology. | SOCIAL SCIENCE / Sociology /
    General. | POLITICAL SCIENCE / Political Freedom & Security / Human Rights.
Classification: LCC HM1251 .J69 2019 | DDC 303.3/6—dc23
LC record available at https://lccn.loc.gov/2019007344

FIRST EDITION
25 24 23 22 21 20 19   10 9 8 7 6 5 4 3 2 1

Production manager: Susan Geraghty
Interior design: Paula Goldstein
Cover design: Dan Tesser, Studio Carnelian
Composition: Westchester Publishing Services
Copyeditor: Michele D. Jones
Proofreader: Cathy Mallon
Indexer: Rebecca Plunkett
Author photo: Matthias Schillig

For each of you who is helping to create a more relational world, whether you're working quietly in the background or marching on the front lines. Thank you.

CONTENTS

Powerarchy

INTRODUCTION

If you find the mirror of the heart dull, the rust has not been cleared from its face.

–RUMI

I was four years old when I began the journey that led to the writing of this book. It was a hot summer day, and I was with my parents on my father's fishing boat, my favorite place in the world to be. And then I caught my first fish.

My parents clapped and laughed and told me how proud they were, but I felt confused and distraught. I didn't understand why I couldn't share their happiness; as I watched the fish I'd pulled out of the ocean flop wildly on the floor of the boat gasping for air, all I could feel was sadness. And guilt.

After that day, my father's boat, once the source of my greatest joy, became a trigger for distress. I couldn't bear to see thrashing fish being pulled off hooks and tossed into a bloody bucket to suffocate. And seafood, which had been my favorite cuisine, sickened me to the point where I could no longer eat it without vomiting.

My emotions and body were reacting to a paradox that my young brain wasn't developed enough to understand. I couldn't reconcile how caring people—my own parents nonetheless—could harm others and neither see nor feel troubled by this contradiction. My parents instilled in me a strong commitment to practicing the Golden Rule—to treating others the way I'd want to be treated if I were in their position. So did my teachers, the ministers at our church, and nearly every adult who influenced my development. Yet it seemed that everywhere I turned, this supposedly highest principle was being violated, and nobody was the least bit concerned.

Whether it was my father killing fish for enjoyment, movies depicting men subduing emotionally distraught women by slapping them across the face (it was the 1960s, after all), or children bullying each other on the playground in plain sight of unconcerned teachers, the relational paradox I was witnessing was the same. The Golden Rule, a principle meant to guide the way we relate to others, was as disregarded as it was esteemed—and, most notably, this contradiction was utterly invisible.

It was more than two decades later that I was finally able to comprehend and articulate this relational paradox, a phenomenon I'd become increasingly sensitized to over the years. I had become deeply concerned with social injustices, and I found myself confounded by the dysfunctional state of humanity that not only allowed for but perpetrated widespread suffering. What, I wondered, makes people turn away from—rather than challenge—atrocities? Why do some of the same people who stand on the streets demonstrating for human rights mistreat members of their own families? Why do those who claim to want a society based on the values of compassion and justice nevertheless vote and act against these values?

The answers to these questions came to me after another incident involving an animal, this time in the form of a hamburger. I was twenty-three years old, and I'd recently eaten a beef patty that was contaminated with campylobacter (the "salmonella" of the red-meat world). I wound up hospitalized and on intravenous antibiotics, and after that experience I found myself too disgusted to eat meat again.

In the process of learning about my new, vegetarian diet, I stumbled upon information about animal agriculture. What I learned shocked and horrified me. The extent of the needless suffering endured by billions of nonhuman animals and the devastation to the environment were almost incomprehensible. But what disturbed me perhaps even more was that nobody I talked to about what I'd learned was willing to hear what I had to say. Their responses were nearly always along the lines of "Don't tell me that;

you'll ruin my meal," or they'd call me a radical vegetarian hippie propagandist. And these were my friends and family—conscientious, rational people who were committed to helping create a more just and compassionate world and who genuinely cared about animals.

THE PSYCHOLOGY OF VIOLENCE
AND NONVIOLENCE

Wanting to understand what it was that caused people to harbor relationally contradictory attitudes and behaviors—what enabled the relational paradox I first observed when I killed the fish—I enrolled in a doctoral program in psychology, where I studied the psychology of violence and nonviolence. What, I asked, enabled caring people to participate in, or otherwise support, practices that harm others, be they human or nonhuman beings? And what, then, could help shift this psychological orientation?

I narrowed the focus of my research to examine a specific expression of the relational paradox: the psychosociology of eating animals, a phenomenon I named *carnism*. Seeking to understand how people who care about the well-being of nonhuman animals nevertheless consume (or kill) them, I conducted interviews and surveys, and coded and analyzed responses. I concluded that eating (certain) animals results from extensive social and psychological conditioning that causes naturally empathic and rational people to distort their perceptions and block their empathy so that they act against their values of compassion and justice without fully realizing what they're doing. In other words, carnism teaches us to violate the Golden Rule without knowing or caring that we're doing so.

What I took away from my research was not simply the discovery of carnism but of how, specifically, violent or oppressive ideologies are structured. I had deconstructed the carnistic system, identifying and articulating the specific social and psychological defense mechanisms that keep it intact. In the process, I realized that these same mechanisms exist in all oppressive systems. In other words, the same psychological (and social) mechanisms that enable us to harm nonhumans enable us to harm humans.

My theory of carnism became popularized through my book *Why We Love Dogs, Eat Pigs, and Wear Cows.* My hope was that the book would not only invite nonvegans to reflect on their relationship with farmed animals but also encourage all people, including vegans, to recognize how various oppressive systems influence the way they relate to others. To some extent, my hope was fulfilled; a number of people shared with me that they found the book applicable across issues and that they had become more conscientious about myriad forms of oppression.

COMPARTMENTALIZING "ISMS" AND RELATIONAL DIMENSIONS

But humans have a remarkable ability to compartmentalize, and vegans are no exception. Just as I was met with resistance by my socially progressive, meat-eating family and friends to my attempts to raise awareness of carnism, I found that a number of vegans reacted defensively to my attempts to raise awareness of feminism, racism, and other oppressions not involving nonhuman animals. I'd point out that, although women make up about 80 percent of the vegan movement, the majority of its leaders are men. I'd also note that vegan outreach doesn't always reflect the experiences and needs of people of color (something vegans of color have been saying for some time),[1] only to have my comments largely disregarded and sometimes argued against—by people who admittedly had little or no literacy, or awareness, around the issues I was raising.

My experience talking about social justice among some vegan advocates paralleled that of my experiences talking about veganism among social justice advocates. It became clear to me that, more often than not, people would step outside of one "ism" only to land (or, rather, remain) in others, while believing they'd somehow extricated themselves from all "isms."

I noticed this same phenomenon occurring across the three dimensions in which people relate: collective/social, interpersonal, and intrapersonal (within and toward oneself). People tend to assume that awareness and transformation in one dimension automatically translate to awareness and transformation in all dimensions. Yet, more often than not, people step out of oppressive or abusive[2] dynamics in one dimension only to stay stuck in such dynamics in one or both of the others. For example, people who are actively working toward more compassionate and just social policies may nevertheless be verbally abusive to those they disagree with, carrying out the same behaviors in the interpersonal dimension that they are challenging in the social dimension.[3]

I realized that it was time for an analysis that seeks to uncover the common denominator among all forms and expressions of oppression: What is the "metasystem," as it were, that envelops all oppressive systems and informs all **relational dimensions**? How do we know we're in it? How does it influence the way we relate to our world, others, and ourselves? And, most important, what can we do to step out of it—or, perhaps more accurately, change our relationship with it?

ABOUT THIS BOOK

This book is the result of my search for answers to the aforementioned questions. In this book, I present a theoretical framework, a model, for helping to understand the nature and structure of oppression from a relational perspective. This framework is based in part on the empirical research I conducted for my doctoral dissertation, as well as on extensions of that analysis that I developed in the following years. But the framework extends well beyond my analysis of carnism. I have synthesized ideas from my work as a psychologist, social justice advocate, relationship specialist, and lecturer in psychological trauma and addictions.[4] Moreover, the ideas in this book have been largely informed by the countless scholars and advocates whose work has been invaluable in illuminating paths to understanding oppression through the fog that obscures it.[5] I draw heavily on the cutting-edge work that informs Relational-Cultural Theory (RCT), developed in large part by Jean Baker Miller, Judith V. Jordan, Janet Surrey, and Irene Stiver from the Wellesley College Stone Center, expanding that theory to include relationships beyond only those between and among humans, and suggesting a model and structure with which to understand all nonrelational systems.

The model I present here is explanatory, in that it offers an explanation of oppression that is intended to enrich existing conversations and encourage further discussion and investigation. This book is not meant to be the primer for transforming oppression, nor is it meant to oversimplify what is clearly a complex problem. Rather, my hope is that the model I present will simply provide a way of understanding oppression that may be helpful as an addition to existing works in this area, an apparatus to include in the existing toolkit of approaches to social transformation, for those for whom it seems useful. (I use examples throughout this book to help clarify the concepts presented. A number of these examples are about male privilege, which is a reflection of my personal experience: I am a former lecturer on feminism and a woman. This focus is not meant to minimize other forms of privilege—many of which I discuss throughout the book—or to imply that males are not also harmed by male privilege and patriarchy, an issue I discuss in upcoming chapters.)

In this book, I propose that there is an overarching belief system that informs all oppressive systems, which I call **powerarchy**.[6] Powerarchy is a nonrelational system that is organized around the belief in a **hierarchy of moral worth**—that some individuals or groups are more worthy of moral consideration than others—and that is structured to maintain unjust power imbalances. Powerarchy reflects and reinforces relational dysfunction—nonrelational power dynamics[7] that violate integrity and harm dignity. Powerarchy exists as a metasystem, as the ethos, or overarching system, that informs oppressive systems in general. It also exists on more discernible levels: powerarchies can be social systems, such as racism and sexism, or interpersonal systems, such as an abusive relationship; and powerarchy informs how we relate to ourselves. In this book, I present an analysis of powerarchy, examining the key psychological and social structures that maintain the system, as well as ways to work toward transformation.

WHO THIS BOOK IS FOR

This book is written with the assumption that readers accept that oppression is a bona fide phenomenon. It is not written for those who are skeptical about the existence of social power imbalances or privileges—both of which are well-documented phenomena.[8] I do not seek to convince readers that, for example, people of color experience widespread injustices or that women have significantly less social power than men. Those who do not have at least some literacy around privilege and oppression will likely be resistant to the ideas presented here, as these ideas build on an understanding of oppressive phenomena, rather than comprehensively explain them. This book is for readers who are concerned about oppression and supportive of progressive social transformation. This book may also appeal to those who wish to understand their experience of power in order to improve their personal lives and relationships.

I believe that a key obstacle to bringing about social transformation swiftly is the lack of a comprehensive, relational framework with which to understand oppression. I believe that the common tendency to view oppressions reductively—as more distinct from one another than they are, and as disconnected across the three relational dimensions of our lives—is in large part due to the fact that we have not fully identified a key common denominator that underlies all forms of oppression.

I wrote this book for those who are doing the vitally important work of helping create a more just and compassionate world. This work is urgent, and I am humbled and inspired by the dedication, effectiveness, and brilliance of the many people who are helping create a better planet for us all. I hope this book will make a contribution to those efforts.

CHAPTER 1

Oppression

A Relational Dysfunction

If we don't get to the root of oppressive behavior, then we risk reproducing the oppressive framework in our own liberation movements.

–SYL KO

Oppression—the unjust allocation and use of power—is arguably the single greatest cause of human and nonhuman suffering and of some of the most perilous environmental problems our planet has ever known.[1] The countless manifestations of oppression range from the seemingly benign to the catastrophic, from the micro (how we treat individuals) to the macro (how we operate as a collective). Rape, war, genocide, child abuse, poverty, environmental degradation, factory farming, terrorism, racism, patriarchy—oppression is manifested in any behavior or system that mirrors and supports the exercising of unjust power and control over another or others.[2] And oppressive behaviors, as well as the attitudes that accompany them, are self-reinforcing: oppression begets oppression, in a feedback loop. So ending oppression—intercepting and transforming the deeply ingrained patterns of thinking and behaving that form the foundation of global suffering and destruction—is arguably the single most important undertaking of our time.

There have been countless efforts to end various forms of oppression over the course of human history; and with increasing awareness of social problems and structural injustices, more and more oppressions are, fortunately, being dismantled. Despite such changes, however, history manages to repeat itself. Often, when one oppression is diminished, a new one emerges or an existing one is bolstered. For example, at the same time that policies are constructed to limit anti-Semitic practices,[3] anti-Muslim behavior is legislated;[4] and although the segregation of black and white people in the US has been abolished, the mass incarceration of black Americans is a growing epidemic.[5] Because we haven't fully identified the deeper principles and structures of oppression—including the psychology that enables it—we've targeted the manifestations of oppression while leaving its core intact, like weeding a garden and leaving the roots behind to fester and proliferate. When we don't understand the broader system, or metasystem, that lies beneath and beyond specific forms of oppression, we risk trading one oppression for another or enabling the same oppression to shapeshift into a new form, even as we work toward social transformation.

Understanding the metasystem of oppression not only prevents us from repeating history but also enables us to more fully and effectively bring about social transformation: it motivates us to unite across social causes so that our efforts become greater than the sum of their parts. For example, although we may choose to focus our energy on ending global poverty, we can at the same time maintain an awareness of the interconnectedness of global poverty and other forms of oppression, such as racism, patriarchy, and nonhuman animal exploitation. We can actively raise awareness of the oppressive mindset that breeds all oppressions, so that regardless of the focus of our social change work, our efforts are contributing toward ending oppression more broadly. We interrupt the wider pattern of oppressive thinking and avoid inadvertently reinforcing the very attitudes, behaviors, and policies that create structural inequalities in the first place.

Understanding the metasystem of oppression also enables us to interrupt and shift the pattern of oppressive thinking and behaving in our personal lives, which is necessary both for the creation of a more just and compassionate world and for our own well-being. The same attitudes and behaviors that enable social oppression and the oppression of nonhuman animals and the environment also enable interpersonal and even intrapersonal **abuse**, and all levels are mutually reinforcing; each feeds the other. When we break the oppressive pattern on any of these levels, we not only cease reinforcing oppression but also help to transform it. (By including the interpersonal and intrapersonal dimensions in my analysis, I do not mean to minimize the very real phenomenon of widespread oppression toward vulnerable groups, a point I discuss throughout this book.)

BEYOND A HIERARCHY OF OPPRESSIONS

Oppressions often exist alongside—rather than above or below—one another. However, many of us who are working toward social transformation tend to think of oppressions in a competitive hierarchy, with some being more worthy of attention than others. (Although from a strategic perspective it is important to consider which causes or oppressions to prioritize, very often arguments about prioritization reflect personal value judgments rather than strategic considerations.) And we may assume that one form of oppression underlies all other forms of oppression—thinking, for example, that if patriarchy or class conflict were abolished, then colonialism would topple.[6] So we can view oppressions like rungs on a ladder, and compete to secure the top position for the oppression about which we are most concerned.

Of course, some oppressions are informed by others. For example, patriarchy gives rise to sexism, heterosexism, and genderism. So patriarchy is the ethos, or the backdrop, from which these other oppressions emerge. However, although patriarchy informs genderism, it does not necessarily give rise to racism or classism. Rather, patriarchy *intersects* with these other oppressions, meaning that it reinforces and is reinforced by them; and together, these oppressions create a distinct social category. (This concept was identified by attorney-activist Kimberle Crenshaw and it's discussed in upcoming chapters.) For example, women of color are more likely than white women or men of color to live in poverty, and as economically disadvantaged women of color, their social experience is distinct from that of economically disadvantaged white women or men of color.[7]

The assumption that oppressions exist in a competitive hierarchy can limit our effectiveness in working toward social change, as those of us working for different causes can end up arguing against one another in an attempt to secure the top rung of the hierarchical ladder, rather than uniting with one another to abolish the very notion of the ladder, a construct that lies at the heart of the metasystem of oppression. (I am not suggesting that hierarchies are inherently problematic. Some hierarchies are natural and necessary. The problem arises when factors that should not be arranged in a hierarchy—such as moral worth—are.) And in our infighting, our respective movements can end up cannibalizing themselves. To be sure, infighting among social justice advocates sometimes reflects differences in opinion that stem from evolving ideas and strategies that can lead to positive change, as when feminists of color challenge the racism of mainstream feminism and demand greater inclusivity. However, challenging ideas is not the same as competing for one's cause to be considered more worthy of attention than others, the latter of which is a mindset that typically leads to destructive fighting, rather than productive growth, among social justice advocates.

Indeed, although different oppressions are experienced differently by their respective victims, the mentality that enables oppression is the same. The same mindset that makes it possible for us to support or tolerate genocides around the world produces and maintains a culture of classist exploitation at home and enables us to justify the confinement of sentient nonhuman animals in factories where their bodies are turned into food. Once we step outside the oppressive mentality, we can appreciate that oppressions are more like spokes on a wheel than rungs on a ladder, with some select spokes branching out into offshoots, and some intersecting with others.

THE MYTH OF A HIERARCHY OF MORAL WORTH

Thinking of oppressions hierarchically can reflect (and reinforce) a belief in a hierarchy of moral worth. It is this very **myth** that forms the foundation of the mindset that drives oppression, the oppressive mentality. The oppressive mentality is a psychological mindset that informs the way people think and feel, and, ultimately, the way they relate.

According to this myth, some individuals or groups are more worthy than others of moral consideration, of being treated with **integrity**—that is, in a way that reflects the core moral values of justice and compassion that are shared across cultures.[8] This hierarchical view of moral worth means that we deny the **dignity**—the inherent worth—of certain individuals or groups. (Dignity is, perhaps not surprisingly, the core concept of the United Nations Universal Declaration of Human Rights, which has laid the foundation for understanding and honoring international social justice.)

The belief in a hierarchy of moral worth is one reason we don't recognize certain individuals as victims of oppression, even when they are; people need to hold a certain moral status in society in order to be recognized as vulnerable to victimization. For example, for decades, psychologists noted that girls and women who were forced by familiars into sexual interaction (a phenomenon we refer to today as being sexually assaulted) subsequently exhibited a number of distressing symptoms. However, rather than recognize such symptoms as indicative of traumatization—of having been over-powered and controlled—psychologists diagnosed the girls and women as "hysterical," as suffering from personal neuroses.[9] It wasn't until the 1970s, when the women's liberation movement had sufficiently elevated the social (and thus moral) status of females,[10] that such symptoms were recognized as hallmarks of posttraumatic stress disorder (PTSD) and that girls and women were acknowledged as victims of such sexual assaults.

When we look at the issue of inherent worth and moral consideration through the lens of psychology, we can appreciate that the belief in a hierarchy of moral worth is deeply dysfunctional and a key driver of oppression. Oppression drives and is driven by a way of relating that is squarely based on the denial of dignity and the violation of integrity. Regardless of who another is or what another has done—whether they are our colleague, our family dog, or a convicted murderer—when we view and treat them in a way that denies their dignity, we demean them and violate our core moral values in the process. Indeed, our psychological, social, and emotional experience is defined and redefined by how we relate—with other humans, with the nonhuman animals with whom we share the planet, and with ourselves—and injuries to our sense of dignity, on the collective and individual levels, lie at the heart of much psychological and relational dysfunction.[11]

Using a psychological lens to look at the belief in a hierarchy of moral worth also helps us see how such a belief is, in fact, inaccurate. Each of us is a composite of the traits and genetic makeup we inherited and our minute-to-minute experiences. The choices we make, the paths we follow, reflect this synthesis of our biology and environment. Expecting that any of us should be different from who and how we are at any given moment is like expecting a tree that's been rained on not to be wet. Some child abuse survivors, for example, go on to be "high achievers" and to break the pattern of abuse in their family systems, while others do not. Perhaps the former group had fewer inherent psychological vulnerabilities or had a positive role model outside the family or had access to information that gave them enough understanding of trauma to be more **resilient**. Any number of factors could have influenced the experience of members of each group such that the trajectories of their lives shifted in one direction or another.

Most of us recognize that factors such as physical appearance, intelligence, and financial power should not be the criteria by which we determine whether someone has inherent worth or deserves moral consideration (even though we don't necessarily act accordingly). However, we have yet to accept that all criteria for such categorization are problematic. This does not mean that we don't hold people accountable for their actions, socially and interpersonally. It simply means that we don't judge anyone as more or less worthy of moral consideration. For example, if we learn of a manager at a company mistreating their coworkers and embezzling money, we may inevitably feel legitimate anger and want them held accountable for their actions—fired from their position and charged with criminal behavior—but we don't have to perceive them as an inferior being. That is to say, we can recognize and respond to problematic behavior without feeling the charge of contempt that signals we've elevated ourselves to a position of moral superiority. We can create more compassionate and just relationships and societies when we honor the dignity of all individuals, even as we work to change harmful attitudes and behaviors.

Moreover, scholars have long debated whether moral consideration should be extended to life beyond humanity. More and more philosophers are recognizing that *speciesism*—the ideology that places animals on a hierarchy of moral worth, with humans at the top—is in fact an expression of human supremacy, an attitude that, when philosophically deconstructed, is like other forms of supremacy and proves to be morally indefensible.[12] Thus the thesis I present in this book includes the assumption that nonhuman beings as individuals (as well as the ecosystems that comprise them)[13] possess inherent worth and are deserving of moral consideration of their interests.

OPPRESSION AS A RELATIONAL PHENOMENON

Although multiple factors, such as powerful economic and other institutional forces, give rise to and help maintain oppression, one key factor, which has only recently begun to receive significant attention, is psychology.[14] In many ways, oppression is a psychological phenomenon; the institutions that sustain oppression are created by and for people, and people are psychological beings. And such institutions and other oppressive structures (e.g., norms and traditions) are in large part driven by, and depend on maintaining, an oppressive mentality.

More precisely, oppression is largely a *relational* phenomenon. Relational dynamics—dynamic interactions that are informed by psychology and that exist between individuals and groups—underlie virtually all human activity. Indeed, for oppression to exist, there must be at least two entities that are in relationship with one another: the oppressor and the oppressed. Oppression reflects and reinforces a relational dysfunction, a pathology in how individuals and social groups relate—to others, the world, and themselves. When we look at the various ways in which oppression is manifested, we can see that they all reflect a way of relating that is inherently damaging to relationships, and often ends up destroying them—and our lives and world are built on relationships. Whether they are brief and benign, enduring and profound, with ourselves or another, between two people or among two million individuals, relationships are a constant: all of us are always in relationship because we are always relating. Indeed, the social systems of which we are a part are themselves simply aggregations of interpersonal dynamics, of relationships.

Most of us recognize relational dysfunction when we see it—for example, between spouses in an unhealthy marriage or among verbally abusive online commentators or warring religious sects. What we typically don't realize is that the same dysfunctional dynamics underlie all problematic relationships, including those played out on the societal stage. A spouse who invalidates and dismisses the experience and needs of their partner is engaging in the same type of dysfunction as an ageist culture that invalidates and dismisses the experiences and needs of older people.

Most of us also recognize relational health when we see it enacted in various personal relationships and social arrangements. Yet we typically don't realize that, for example, a spouse who honors their partner's dignity—who treats their partner as though they are inherently worthy and thus deserve to be empathized with, to be treated fairly, and to feel safe[15]—is engaging in the same healthy relational dynamic as that of a society that encourages policies and practices that honor the dignity of members of more vulnerable groups while also seeking to empower such groups so that they are no longer vulnerable in the first place.

Despite the central role that psychology (and, by extension, relationality) plays in enabling oppression, those working toward social transformation rarely give it the attention it deserves.[16] Discussions about social change have typically been centered around ideology and philosophy. Ideological considerations tend to focus on content—on what end, what kind of system, to work toward (e.g., democracy or benevolent dictatorship, capitalism or socialism). Philosophical considerations sometimes also focus on ends, but they address the process, or the means, as well. One critical philosophical consideration is the question of whether an ethical end justifies unethical means: Is it ethical, for instance, to use weapons to create a less violent social order—to use the same tools to try to end oppression that helped create the oppression in the first place? Such questions remain unanswered when not also looked at through the lens of psychology. Approaching ideology or philosophy as devoid of psychology is like approaching language as devoid of grammar: words alone are not enough to create a coherent and productive conversation.

If we wish to transform oppression, we must understand the psychology, the mentality, that underlies all oppressions and that is causing us to wreak havoc on humanity, devastate billions of nonhuman animals, and destroy our very planet. We must also understand the relational dynamics this mentality gives rise to. As authors Aph and Syl Ko point out, we can't create effective liberation movements without understanding the anatomy of oppression.[17] Transforming oppression requires not simply the abolition of oppressive policies and practices but the transformation of the way we think and, ultimately, relate. Thus, it requires an understanding of the psychological processes that inform our relationships with ourselves and others so that we can shift from operating within a (largely unconscious) dysfunctional and nonrelational model to living consciously within one that is healthy and empowering. Examining and deconstructing the oppressive mentality and its manifestations, and illuminating its alternative, is the focus of this book, and we'll discuss specific strategies for change in chapters 7 and 8.

RELATIONALITY AND RELATIONAL BEHAVIORS

To help cultivate healthier relationships in our lives and world, we need to understand what relationality is—specifically, what relational (and nonrelational) behaviors and dynamics look like. We also need to appreciate how relational and nonrelational behaviors are informed by, and inform, the systems of which we are a part.

There is a growing body of research on relationality.[18] However, for our purposes—understanding relationality across all three relational dimensions—perhaps the most notable research comes from the field of Relational-Cultural Theory (RCT). RCT holds that relationships lie at the core of individual and social functioning, and that healthy relationships, which comprise **healthy relational behaviors**,[19] are essential for individual and social well-being. Other significant research on relationality comes from attachment theory, which holds that the way we attach to others is central to how we view and behave toward others and ourselves.[20]

Healthy relational behaviors are those that create a sense of connection and foster a sense of security and mutual **empowerment** (factors that we'll discuss more fully in upcoming chapters). They reflect the practice of integrity[21] and honor the dignity of all participants. In contrast, **nonrelational behaviors** create a sense of disconnection and foster a sense of insecurity and **disempowerment.** They violate integrity and harm dignity.

Although the prevailing assumption among psychologists in most societies has been that healthy psychological functioning requires a high degree of autonomy, this individualistic model has been increasingly challenged. Numerous studies have shown that humans are both inherently and highly relational: we're hardwired to need connection with others, and we're harmed by the experience of disconnection.[22] Indeed, we thrive, both emotionally and neuropsychologically, when we feel secure and **empowered** in our relationships, and we are negatively impacted, psychologically and biologically, by affronts to our dignity—by behaviors that deny our inherent worth.

Moreover, fascinating new research on the neuropsychology of attachment suggests that our *attachment style*, the way we attach to others, has a profound impact on many critical aspects of our personal and relational experience: it helps determine our capacity for trust and empathy, our ability to feel secure in (nonthreatening) relationships and within ourselves, and our capacity for intimacy.[23] In addition, our attachment style influences whether we are attuned to our needs and the needs of others, and whether we validate and respond to those needs (when healthful and appropriate); whether we tend to be controlling, insensitive, or defensive; and whether we respect our boundaries and the boundaries of others. Perhaps most notably, our attachment style helps determine our sense of self-worth and our perception of the worth of others, as well as whether or not we honor such worth.

When our attachment style is *insecure*, we are more likely to engage in nonrelational behaviors, by either directing them toward others or allowing others to direct them toward us, or both. We tend to have lower self-worth and therefore to be more defensive against constructive criticism, perceiving it as an affront to our dignity. We tend to feel either inferior or superior to others and to act accordingly. When our attachment style is *secure*, we are more likely to engage in relational behaviors. We have a healthier sense of self-worth, feeling neither superior nor inferior to others, and we tend to be more receptive to information that challenges us to grow.

Although our attachment style is largely the result of our hardwiring and our earliest experiences with our primary caregivers, research suggests that it is also affected, and can even be changed, by relationships throughout the course of our life.[24] So our attachment style influences and is influenced by that of others, for better or worse. And although actually switching our attachment style is believed to result from a more prolonged and/or intense relationship, casual interpersonal dynamics, particularly if such dynamics are prevalent—enacted by multiple individuals and carried out repeatedly—may nevertheless push us along the attachment spectrum in one direction or another. Moreover, because neither individuals nor relationships exist in a vacuum, the systems of which we are a part—systems that are themselves composed of myriad relationships—may play a role in shaping our attachment style.[25]

Looking at a system through the lens of attachment is one way we might assess whether the system is healthful or dysfunctional—whether it is relational or nonrelational. And it should come as no surprise that systems which cultivate and reflect insecure attachment are oppressive. Oppressive systems may well create the very conditions—intrapersonally, interpersonally, and socially—that damage a core driver of personal and relational well-being: our ability to attach securely.

OPPRESSION AND ABUSE

In order to work toward improved relational well-being, social and interpersonal, it is important to recognize the similarities and differences between oppression and abuse. Oppression is the unjust allocation and use—the abuse—of power. Social or collective unjust allocations and abuses of power are usually referred to as "oppression," and interpersonal ones, including those that occur in groups such as families or workplaces, are usually referred to as "abuse." In all cases, however, the dynamic—the way of interacting—is the same: an unbalanced allocation of power and the process of abusing power that enable social oppression also enable interpersonal abuse. (Similar abusive dynamics can sometimes be carried out intrapersonally. When I refer to interpersonally abusive dynamics in this book, often the same points apply to intrapersonal dynamics, though I won't always note that this is the case.)

However, oppression and abuse are of course not identical phenomena. Although the psychological process that underlies each phenomenon is often the same, oppression and abuse differ in two key ways.

First, oppression is always systemic—embedded within a system—whereas abuse can be either an isolated behavior or systemic, existing within a relationship or group where there is an imbalance of power (such as between that of a batterer and their partner or between a boss and a subordinate). Many people will, for example, occasionally engage in abusive behavior, as when in the midst of a heated argument an angry spouse says things they know will hurt their partner. Although problematic, this kind of behavior is not necessarily part of a pattern that informs a system. In an abusive system, the abuser consistently holds power over the other, and this imbalance of power creates the dynamic which mirrors that of oppressive dynamics.[26] For example, even during so-called good times, an abusive spouse may still wield power and control over their partner by doing things such as soliciting information about the partner's vulnerabilities that the abuser can later use against them. In an abusive system, the powerholder seeks to maintain and often grow the power imbalance within the system, to hold power and control over the other; abuse is just a means to that end.[27]

The second difference between abuse and oppression is that, unlike abuse, oppression is institutionalized, in that it is embraced and maintained by all major social institutions. This is why there is no such thing as "reverse oppression." Oppression, by definition, must be housed within a system in which there is an unjust allocation—an unfair imbalance—of power on the societal, or social level. So although some women can, for example, act abusively to men, they cannot *oppress* men, because women have less social power than men.

Often, oppressive dynamics inform abusive ones. Social scientists and social change agents are well aware of how *social power relations*—the dynamic between social groups when one has more power than the other, as with men and women—trickle down to influence *interpersonal power relations*, the dynamic between individuals when one has more power than the other. For example, in the 1960s, feminists pointed out how institutionalized patriarchy—the socially sanctioned oppression of women and girls that is manifested through sexist attitudes, behaviors, and policies—was a cause of men abusing women in interpersonal relationships. Both men and women had been conditioned to believe that husbands had the right to control their wives; therefore a number of married men engaged in abusive and controlling behaviors, and their wives didn't recognize such behaviors as abusive and simply accepted them as normal and appropriate.[28]

Conversely, when we abuse power interpersonally, we contribute to a broader collective dysfunction, because we as individuals make up the broader society. Obviously, the influence of social power relations on individuals is far greater than vice versa. However, on both levels—social and interpersonal—the process of abusing power is mutually reinforcing: each level feeds the other, and the difference is a matter of degree.

POWERARCHY: THE METASYSTEM OF OPPRESSION

I propose that oppression results, in large part, from the synthesis of a **power dynamic** (a relational dynamic based on a particular model of power) and a system that provides the structure, or guidelines, for enacting the power dynamic. This combination creates a particular type of system that I refer to as a *powerarchy*. Powerarchies are fundamentally nonrelational; their core premise—that moral worth exists on a hierarchy—and the power dynamics that reflect and reinforce this premise are relationally dysfunctional. Powerarchies damage relationships, and they violate the integrity and harm the dignity of the individuals within them. Powerarchies cause us to violate the first precept of relating, the Golden Rule, and in so doing, they lie at the heart of the relational paradox described in the introduction.

This model for understanding oppression is thus *relational*. It examines how oppression informs and is informed by human interaction in all three relational dimensions: social/collective,[29] interpersonal, and intrapersonal.[30] It is *inclusive* as well, because, although it is grounded in psychology, it includes ideological and philosophical considerations; it also includes in its analysis how humans relate to nonhuman animals and the environment, something other models of oppression have largely failed to do. Moreover, the model is *descriptive*; it describes the defensive structures and strategies that uphold oppression in relation to one another. And, finally, it is *explanatory*, in that it seeks to explain oppression—from a relational perspective—while recognizing that such an explanation is building on those that came before and paving the way for further discussion and investigation. [31]

• • •

The good news is that just as oppression begets oppression, so too does liberation beget liberation. So when we understand the nature and structure of powerarchy, we have a deeper understanding not only of oppression but also of liberation. And we can work more fully toward transformation for ourselves, others, and our world.

CHAPTER 2

The Process of Power

Power over others is weakness disguised as strength.
–ECKHART TOLLE

A powerful man is believed to have said, "Make the lie big, make it simple, keep saying it, and eventually they will believe it."[1] And an even more powerful man is believed to have said, "All through history the way of truth . . . [has] always won. There have been tyrants and murderers . . . but in the end, they always fall. Think of it—always."[2] Both of these individuals were world leaders who used their power to change the course of history. But they were operating from within very different models of power. Hitler was operating from within a nonrelational model based on dominance and control, whereas Gandhi was operating from within a relational model based on integrity and dignity. One used his power to oppress, the other to liberate.

It is not only world leaders whose power may be used toward harm or healing. Each of us is continually engaged in power dynamics, behavioral interactions in which our power may be used toward one end or the other. These power dynamics can reflect and reinforce the problematic model of power that supports oppression, or they can help us work toward creating healthier relationships and a more just society.

If we are aware of the deeper psychological structures that give rise to power dynamics, we are better able to be intentional, rather than reactive, when we engage in these interactions. Understanding what power is, the process of how we use or exercise our power, and the models of power on which our process is based can help ensure that we use our power toward liberation rather than to support the powerarchical status quo.

WHAT IS POWER?

Power is the capacity or ability to influence others, oneself, or events to bring about a desired outcome.[3] Basically, when we have power, we are able to exert our will in order to get what we want.

Of course, sometimes we have power, but don't feel **powerful**.[4] One reason is that we may not be aware of the power we have. For example, even if we have plenty of money, we may also have a "mentality of poverty." So we may not feel financially empowered,[5] meaning that we don't feel that we have the power to take financial action. Another reason we may not feel as powerful as we are is that we have low self-worth—we feel that we don't have sufficient value as a person. Indeed, our sense of self-worth can inform, to a significant degree, our perception of our power,[6] as illustrated in the all-too-common example of an individual not feeling worthy and thus empowered enough to leave a problematic relationship. In other words, when our self-worth is low, so too may be our perception of our power and, therefore, our sense of empowerment (our ability to act or influence). Conversely, an inflated sense of self-worth can result in our feeling more powerful than we actually are, such as when, for example, a narcissistic executive behaves recklessly and unethically, thinking they're above reproach.

Moreover, just as our sense of self-worth can influence our perception of our power, so too can our perception of our power influence our sense of self-worth. For example, when we feel that we have the ability to influence others, events, or ourselves, we can feel better about ourselves, more worthy. It's also possible to feel powerful in one sense, but not in another. For example, we may feel powerful in our role as CEO of an organization and have a high level of professional confidence, but we may nevertheless lack self-worth and struggle to feel a sense of empowerment in other roles, such as when we are a partner in an intimate relationship.

THE "WAY" OF POWER

Most social scientific research on power focuses on two key questions: How is power exercised, or used? and For what purpose is it used? In other words, social scientists are largely interested in the *process*[7] **of power**, or the *way* that we use and experience our power and the power of others, particularly when we're interacting.[8]

Every interaction has two parts: the *content* and the *process*. The content is the topic, what we are interacting about, and the process is the method, how we are interacting. The process includes our behaviors and, often, our motivations for engaging in the behaviors and in the interaction as a whole. Are we, for example, listening and open to the other's point of view and needs, with the objective of reaching mutual understanding? Or are we interrupting and simply trying to prove the rightness of our position to get our way? Are we respecting the power we have in the interaction, or are we abusing it?

Indeed, the process of an interaction may even be contradictory to the content we're discussing: we could be talking about the importance of justice while engaging in a process that is unjust—perhaps publicly assaulting the character of someone whose politics we disagree with. This is, in fact, a common occurrence and is one reason why advocates for a just cause may struggle to win supporters.

Although the content of an interaction certainly matters, the process may matter more. For example, we tend to more easily forget the content than the process of a communication: after conversing, we may not even remember *what* we talked about, but we may well recall how we *felt* during the conversation.

It is at the level of process where oppressive ways of relating—dysfunctional, abusive power dynamics—are either reinforced or transformed, internally and externally and personally and socially.

When therapists work with families or couples in distress and when political mediators work with heads of state in conflict, their main job is to attend to the process of interactions between the two parties so that healing and reconciliation may begin.

POWER MODELS

The process that informs our power dynamics reflects and reinforces the model of power within which we are operating. This **power model** is a framework, a guide for how and why to use our power, including how to increase our sense of power.

Although social scientists hold a variety of perspectives on what kinds of power models exist, these perspectives tend to fall into two categories,[9] reflecting the two models mentioned earlier. One model is dysfunctional and disempowering[10] and the other is functional and empowering. One is disconnecting and the other leads to greater connection within ourselves and between ourselves and others.[11] One harms self-worth and the other helps enhance it. One fuels powerarchy and the other offsets it.

Social scientists refer to these models as the *dominance* model, also referred to as the **power-over model** (for simplicity, I use only "power over" to denote this model), and the *functionalist* model,[12] which is very similar to what some theorists have referred to as the **power-with model**. I therefore use the terms *functionalist* and *power with* interchangeably, to describe a model that is a hybrid of these two perspectives.[13] The power-over model, of course, is that which informs, and is informed by, powerarchy.

The model of power we employ determines, to a large extent, what we experience and create in our lives and our world. Indeed, every interaction we engage in—with the woman sitting next to us on the bus, with our life partner, with our companion animal, with our elected officials, or with ourselves (through, for example, our *internal dialogue*, or our inner self-talk; or our life choices)—reflects and reinforces one of these models.

It's helpful to think of these power models on a spectrum rather than dualistically, with power over on one end and power with on the other. So an interaction, or power dynamic, need not be reduced to either dysfunctional or functional, disconnecting or connecting, but can be more or less so.

POWER OVER (THE DOMINANCE MODEL)

Power-over behaviors[14] are those in which power is used to exert dominance and control over others, either overtly or subtly. In the power-over model, we place our interests over those of others or of the relationship of which we are a part. In other words, we use our power to get what we want, to serve our own ends, without regard for the interests of others. We either disregard others' interests apathetically, or we intentionally violate them. For example, a stockholder of an oil company may vote against a political initiative to increase support for green energy, not because they *want* to harm the environment, but because they don't care about harming it or they care less about harming the environment than they do about harming their own profits. Or that same stockholder may vote against such an initiative with the intention to harm a green energy company that's run by a colleague they dislike.

In the power-over model, we may also use our power in order to increase our feeling of being powerful by demonstrating to others and/or to ourselves that we have power. (When a feeling or behavior is witnessed, it is validated and can therefore feel more potent.) For example, perhaps the stockholder voted against the initiative not to achieve the practical end they desire—more profits—but to demonstrate that they have the power to help block such an initiative, thus increasing their feeling of being powerful. (As mentioned in note 4, increased levels of dopamine have been associated with the "high" of feeling powerful, so some researchers have suggested that feeling powerful may be addictive.)

In the power-over model, we may use our power not simply to feel more powerful but to feel more worthy. In other words, we sometimes use our power in order to increase our sense of self-worth, often at the expense of others' sense of self-worth—we may view and treat others as inferior so that we don't feel inferior ourselves. Social scientists have noted how individuals who feel inferior and ashamed try to defend themselves against acknowledging these feelings by deprecating others.[15] Individuals who suffer from narcissistic personality disorder are perhaps a prime example of such a phenomenon: they engage in self-serving, power-over behaviors that are often demeaning to others, and need constant affirmation and adulation from others, because they feel fundamentally unworthy. Indeed, the power-over model reflects and reinforces the belief in a hierarchy of moral worth, the central myth that upholds powerarchy. We are more likely to use our power at the expense of others when we perceive them as less worthy of moral consideration; and when we use our power at the expense of others, we reinforce the perception that they are less worthy of moral consideration.

When we use power over to increase our feeling of being more worthy, we can end up feeling even less so than we had originally. For example, imagine a college student proudly telling his girlfriend (who is also a student) that he got a B on a difficult math exam, and his girlfriend replies, "I don't know what you're so excited about. It's not like you got an A." He then replies, "Well, at least I didn't get a C on my English 101 term paper!" to which his girlfriend retorts, "At least *I* didn't fail an entire semester because I was too depressed to get myself to class!" and so on, in a never-ending cycle of degradation. Eventually, one of the partners will deliver the zinger that hits the other's sense of self-worth hard enough that they back down, likely feeling devastated. For a moment, the winner may feel a sense of inflated power, gloating in their success, but at some point, their guilt will creep in, and they will probably feel ashamed of having demeaned their partner. On some level, the winner knows that succeeding at degrading others is no success at all and that the win-lose model is, in reality, lose-lose.

Indeed, power over is individualistic rather than relational, as power is used to satisfy individual interests without regard for the interests of others or of the greater good of the relationship within which the individuals are operating. Individualistic models tend to be competitive: when people see themselves (and their interests) as separate from others, they will tend to try to distinguish themselves from others and also to ensure that their own interests are the ones that get met. For this reason, power over has also been referred to as "competitive power."

On a psychological level, the competitive aspect of power over often manifests through comparison: we feel more or less powerful (e.g., beautiful, wealthy, ethical, intelligent) based on how we compare to others, how much more power we have in a given area than they do.[16] When our sense of self-worth is dependent on factors outside ourselves and often beyond our control, we tend to feel insecure and out of control, whether we realize it or not, and we end up needing ongoing boosts to our sense of worth. So we have to keep searching for more comparisons to keep our self-worth propped up. The power-over model is organized around winners and losers, haves and have-nots. One cannot exist without the other, and in this model, we strive to be the former, usually at the expense of others and always at the expense of our integrity—the practicing of our core moral values of compassion and justice—because we act against these values whenever we diminish others. Individualistic models also tend toward dualistic, or black-and-white, thinking. When we perceive ourselves as separate and distinct from others, we tend to think in terms of "either-or" rather than "both-and." We may therefore place individuals and groups into rigid categories in our minds, whereby they lose nuance: we see others (and ourselves) as either good or bad, right or wrong, a perpetrator or a victim or a hero. We lose the ability to recognize that good people engage in harmful behaviors, that we can be a perpetrator *and* a victim *and* a hero.

Power-over behaviors are inherently disconnecting. We feel disconnected from others when we compete with them and define ourselves as better than they are, because this behavior causes us to be less likely to identify with them (to see something of ourselves in them and something of them in ourselves) and therefore less likely to empathize with them. It is much easier to see someone as a "loser" or a "have-not" when we don't feel what they are feeling. And when our identification and empathy are diminished, so too is our desire and ability to act with compassion. For example, when we perceive our politically conservative sister-in-law as a fundamentally different kind of person than we are, we are more likely to say things to (and about) her that don't take her feelings into account. So the power-over model leads to **othering**—to seeing others as fundamentally different from and inferior to ourselves—which forms the foundation of prejudice.[17] Moreover, when we participate in power-over dynamics intrapersonally, we feel disconnected from ourselves. When we engage in self-degradation, such as telling ourselves we're "stupid" or "lazy," we're empathizing less with ourselves, and we therefore feel less compassion for ourselves. We also feel disconnected from ourselves, because when we exercise power over, we typically violate our integrity—we disconnect from our core values—an issue we will discuss shortly.

PHYSICAL AND PSYCHOLOGICAL POWER OVER AND DISEMPOWERMENT

In its extreme expression, power over reflects the dynamics of domination and subjugation, of one individual or group exercising total power and control over another individual or group. Consider, for example, the dynamics of rape, genocide, slavery, and nonhuman animal exploitation. All power and control have been taken from the victims. This results in their **physical disempowerment**, whereby they lack the ability to act or influence; and in some cases in their **psychological disempowerment**, whereby they lack the *belief* in their ability to act or influence (which often, though not always, includes a diminished sense of self-worth).

When we exercise physical power over another, we use physical means (or practical means, such as money) to overpower or control them, rendering them **disempowered**. When we exercise psychological power over another, we use psychological means toward the same end, often by getting them to distrust their own perceptions, to question the truth of their experience—in essence, to see themselves through our eyes and to trust our perceptions over their own. As a result, their sense of self-control, confidence, and often self-worth may be replaced with self-doubt, insecurity, and shame.

Even when power over is expressed primarily through physical means, it nearly always causes some degree of psychological disempowerment as well. It is almost impossible for someone being raped, for example, to resist internalizing the message that they are not worthy of respect as their body is being overpowered and violated.[18] Moreover, psychological disempowerment is usually a necessary prerequisite for obtaining full power and control over another or others;[19] people's automatic impulse is to resist being overpowered and controlled, so they must be coerced into participating in their own oppression, often by being convinced that they are not worthy of being treated justly. For example, many cult leaders convince their followers to distrust their own perceptions and feelings and to believe that their self-worth comes from acting in accordance with the dictates of the cult.[20] Thus the cult members are far more receptive to being physically controlled, and they are less likely to resist being treated harshly for deviating from the rules of the cult. (I do not mean to imply that individuals are in any way responsible for their victimization, but rather to point out how the process of victimization often causes individuals to unwittingly act against their own interests.)

Sometimes, power-over behaviors are not enacted in order to demean or to otherwise cause unnecessary harm, but are simply the result of automatic responses to stimuli. Most notable of such behaviors are those in which our prefrontal cortex, the region of our brain that enables us to make rational decisions, has been bypassed.

Our behaviors are thus the result of neurochemical reactions that are not in our control, as when we are reacting to an immediate threat to our physical safety or we are reacting because of a condition such as posttraumatic stress disorder (PTSD). Indeed, our brains are hardwired to engage in power-over behaviors when necessary, and these behaviors have performed an important evolutionary function, helping preserve the well-being of groups, communities, and humanity by ensuring that potential threats to oneself or one's group were readily perceived and reacted to.

Functionalist social scientists, such as Dachner Kelter, author of *The Power Paradox*, have pointed out that although power-over behaviors were once necessary for human survival, today, given the evolution of complex social organization and social intelligence, such behaviors are largely dysfunctional.[21] Looking at the construction of leadership, they point out how, in complex modern societies, lasting power must be earned rather than taken by brute force. Power is not bestowed upon those who dominate but rather is given to those who build relationships within the group, advancing the interests of all members of the group. Of course, corrupt leaders exist, and power can corrupt even the most ethical leaders. And, as noted, power-over behaviors are to some degree hardwired. However, functionalist social scientists hold that, rather than serving to protect and preserve groups, power-over behaviors tend to harm groups. Moreover, given the development of social intelligence, we are no longer fully at the mercy of our reptilian brain and can make conscious, intentional choices about how to act, rather than operate on instinct. We have also evolved to be able to make choices that reflect long-term considerations, rather than a short-sighted drive for instant gratification. Human (and planetary) well-being depends on behaviors that serve the interests of not merely the individual but all stakeholders and, ultimately, the greater good of the group or relationship. These behaviors are reflected and reinforced by the power-with model.

POWER WITH (THE FUNCTIONALIST MODEL)

Unlike the power-over model, which reflects and reinforces the belief in a hierarchy of moral worth, the power-with model reflects and reinforces the belief that all individuals are equal in inherent worth, that they possess the same essential dignity. Thus all individuals are recognized as equally deserving of moral consideration.

Power-with behaviors are those in which power is used in the service of the whole—of the greater good of the relationship or group. Power-with behaviors foster mutual relational empowerment[22] (the ability to act or influence in ways that are relationally healthful), connection, and enhanced self-worth. In the power-with model, when we use our power, we take into account the impact of our choices on others, and act in the best interest of the whole. We strengthen our sense of empowerment and self-worth by helping others strengthen theirs. We therefore feel more connected with others—psychologically, because we identify with them, and emotionally, because we empathize with them. And we feel more connected with ourselves, both because we self-empathize more and because when we act in accordance with our core moral values, we feel more internal unity—our values and practices are more connected, more aligned.

Indeed, the power-with model is organized around integrity, because acting in the interests of all parties to cultivate a healthy relationship or group dynamic requires the behaviors that reflect integrity—behaviors that foster, for instance, trust, security, connection, and awareness. Integrity is the integration of core moral values and practices. It is practicing what we preach. For example, if we value justice (being fair to others), we practice integrity when we treat others the way we would want to be treated. If we treat others differently, then we violate our integrity. Integrity is a practice, a road map for guiding our behaviors to ensure that they lead to greater overall empowerment and connection.

As mentioned in chapter 1, the core moral values that integrity is based on include, most notably, compassion and justice.[23]

The practice of these values is supported by the practice of curiosity, honesty, and courage. *Compassion* is having an open heart and truly caring about the well-being of others and of ourselves, and it is also acting on that caring—such as when a competitive sibling chooses to praise his brother's achievements or when "ordinary" people come together in the aftermath of a natural disaster to provide relief for those in need. *Justice* is doing to others as we would have others do to us (and treating them as we imagine they would want to be treated, given what we understand of them)—and vice versa, for those of us who tend to treat others better than we treat ourselves. *Curiosity* is having an open mind, genuinely seeking understanding—such as when arguing partners pause and truly hear each other's point of view, or if the dominant white culture in the United States were to listen to and acknowledge the claims of Native Americans, whose voices have been silenced and whose history has been largely erased. *Honesty* is not simply about telling the truth but also about seeing the truth. Honesty is not denying or avoiding important truths, even if those truths are painful to face—such as when a parent opens their eyes to the reality that their child is addicted to drugs or when the Germans acknowledged the genocide perpetrated in their name and constructed programs and policies to help prevent history from repeating itself. *Courage* is the willingness to be, for example, honest and curious even when doing so feels frightening or threatening; it is the willingness to be vulnerable with others and with ourselves.

When we practice integrity by acting out these core values, the situation is usually—perhaps always—win-win. What increases my integrity helps you increase yours. What enhances the integrity of a relationship helps enhance the integrity of everyone in that relationship. And when each individual practices integrity, the integrity of the world expands. So a useful guiding question when making any kind of relational or social decision is, "What would increase my integrity?" or "What would enhance the integrity of the relationship or the world?" For example, perhaps we speak up to interrupt the process of power over when a group of men are commenting about their female colleagues' bodies or sexuality or are making otherwise sexist comments. Pointing out the sexist behavior reinforces our integrity and encourages the others to practice theirs. It also helps increase integrity on the societal level, because we've disrupted problematic patriarchal attitudes and behaviors.

Power with can be understood as practicing our integrity by making it easier for others to practice theirs. And (as with power over) practicing power with creates a feedback loop: the more we do it, the more we increase the chances that we, and others, will continue to be relational rather than dysfunctional.

Indeed, power with is the practice of love. In his seminal book, *The Road Less Traveled*, psychiatrist M. Scott Peck contends that love is not merely a feeling; it is also an action.[24] Peck says that the behavior of love is acting in the best interests of another, which is essentially practicing integrity—or power with.

Practicing power with ultimately helps us evolve toward our highest and deepest selves because it helps bring us into a state of **mindfulness**, or **presence**. When we are in a state of presence, we are in the moment. We do not ruminate about the future or lament the past; rather, we mindfully focus our **awareness** on others' and our own current unfolding experience. We feel connected with others and ourselves through our empathy and compassion—through our recognition of our shared capacity for suffering and mortality as well as our shared dignity.[25] Presence is a state of being that many of the most renowned philosophers, spiritual teachers, and psychologists refer to as our ideal and most highly evolved state.

SHAME AND GRANDIOSITY VERSUS PRIDE AND HUMILITY

Power over reflects and reinforces shame and grandiosity. **Shame** is the feeling of being less than—and, more specifically, of being less worthy than—others. Unlike guilt, which reflects how we feel about a behavior, shame reflects how we feel about ourselves, our very being. Conversely, **grandiosity** is the feeling of being better than—or more worthy than—others. Shame is feeling inferior; grandiosity is feeling superior. Both shame and grandiosity result from the core belief of powerarchy, the belief in a hierarchy of moral worth, and they drive many of our problematic interpersonal and social dynamics.

Shame results from and causes violations of integrity, in a vicious cycle. When we feel shame, we are less likely to pay attention to and practice integrity because our focus is on self-defense, on preventing ourselves from feeling further shamed. Shame can make us feel as though we're emotionally drowning, so we grab for anything that floats; and, often, we push others under in the process. For example, imagine that a young man who has recently started dating another man reveals to his new romantic interest that his feelings are growing and that he wants to make a more serious commitment. The other, however, expresses some ambivalence and asks for more time to consider what direction he would like the relationship to go in. The young man may feel rejected and therefore ashamed. He may be tempted to avoid the other's phone calls or to make it clear that he's actively pursuing other potential love interests. These actions are designed to protect his sense of self-worth and possibly even to make the other man question his, so that the young man feels more worthy by comparison.

Shame is arguably the foundation of human psychological dysfunction and, by extension, social dysfunction.[26] The essential human need to feel worthy is so powerful, and shame so disruptive to our psychological security and well-being, that we often will do just about anything to avoid this feeling: we may accumulate millions of dollars, sculpt our physical image to fit a cultural ideal of beauty, or become a paragon of success in the areas that matter to us, and we may do so at the expense of others.[27] Indeed, wars have been waged in defense of honor—that is, in an attempt to offset shame—and in some cultures, suicide is considered a better alternative to having one's shame exposed.

To feel shame is to feel that the core of who we are is flawed, not good enough, invalid. And because feeling shame is itself shameful (we feel ashamed of being ashamed), we tend to hide our shame from others and even from ourselves. We pretend it doesn't exist: we bury it under endless piles of work, wrap it inside our achievements, and tuck it away beneath the layers of distractions that keep us continually focused outside ourselves. We act as if we feel good enough, perhaps even superior, when inside we are self-doubting and feeling like an imposter. In our relationships, we may act as if we don't care and withhold words of affection, when what we really want is for the other to tell us how much they love us.

Shame is also a powerful means of social control: members of groups with less social power are often conditioned to feel ashamed of their situation and of themselves for being in it, rather than to feel the motivating emotion of anger, which would be a more appropriate reaction to the injustice of their circumstances. For example, Americans whose native language is English often raise their voice (usually in frustration) when speaking with immigrants who don't understand what they're saying, as though the immigrants were "hard of hearing" rather than struggling against a language barrier. The immigrants frequently feel ashamed of themselves for their lack of understanding, believing that the other's annoyance is justified and that the inability to communicate is due to their own shortcomings—to their lack of English proficiency. More likely, though, such communication breakdown is caused by the (probably monolingual) native English speaker, who lacks an understanding of the appropriate means of communicating with nonnative speakers. Also more likely is that the native English speaker's irritation and raised voice reflect not justifiable anger but disrespect, probably stemming from racism and/or nationalism. Were the immigrants to realize these facts and to appreciate that they have an equal right to occupy the same space as the native English speaker (whose family are also most likely immigrants; it's just a matter of how many generations back), their shame would no doubt be replaced by anger.

Shaming others is a counterproductive means of encouraging positive change in their attitudes and behaviors. Indeed, research has demonstrated that people typically respond to being shamed by engaging in defensive, power-over dynamics; they are less likely to think rationally and act compassionately.[28] So if we want people to respond to requests (or even demands) for positive change, we must make such requests in a way that honors the dignity of those being challenged, while nevertheless raising awareness of the problems they've caused and holding them accountable for those problems. Of course, some people in some situations respond to being shamed by making positive changes. However, it is likely that such a response is *in spite* of, rather than *because* of, having been shamed. Moreover, people can feel ashamed even when they are not being shamed, but this doesn't negate the importance of avoiding the use of shame as a tactic to encourage positive change.

Grandiosity is often a mask for shame. Consider the boy who falls down on the playground and is teased (shamed) for crying over his scraped knee. He pulls himself up, puffs out his chest, and punches at his bullies in an "I'll show you" display of force. The shamed becomes the shamer, perpetuating a cycle that is, unfortunately, a hallmark of many interactions and relationships. Or consider how some working-class white people, who, feeling inferior compared to their more educated or financially advantaged counterparts, may degrade and bully people of color, who provide a convenient "other" against whom they may position themselves as superior.

Indeed, beneath all our striving to feel powerful, in control, beautiful, successful, and so on, what each of us truly wants is to feel that we are enough, that we are worthy. We want to feel that regardless of what we do, it is who we are, intrinsically, that matters. We want to feel **pride**. Healthy pride is not the expression of an inflated ego but rather the recognition that we are fundamentally worthy. Pride is feeling not less worthy than, but as worthy as, others. Pride is the opposite of shame. It is the essence of personal and social well-being, just as shame is the foundation of personal and social dysfunction. Pride motivates us to take positive action on behalf of ourselves and others. This is one reason why social justice movements often seek to cultivate pride in their proponents. For example, in the US in the 1960s and 1970s, the black pride movement sought to transform the internal experience of black people so that they would feel empowered to transform the external power structures that kept them oppressed.

Perhaps not surprisingly, then, practicing power with helps transform shame into pride. Shame is incompatible with integrity, and practicing power with enhances integrity. Integrity brings us into connection with ourselves, others, and our values. One indication that we are in a power-with dynamic is that we feel an absence or alleviation of shame.

And as pride is the opposite of shame, **humility** is the opposite of grandiosity. Humility is the recognition that we are not more worthy than others but (as with pride) as worthy as they are. When we are both proud and humble, we recognize our own worth and appreciate the worth of others. We recognize the inherent worth of other beings with whom we share the planet, and our practices and policies reflect this understanding.

Shame and grandiosity are relational emotions: they exist only in relationship, as they result from comparison—even if the comparison is simply internal, based on a distorted image of ourselves. For example, we may feel ashamed because we don't measure up to our own self-created ideal of who or how we believe we should be. Pride and humility, however, can exist independent of a relational dynamic, as they are not based on comparison or external factors, though they can also be inspired by power-with interactions.

TRAUMA AND ADDICTION VERSUS LOVE AND PRESENCE

Power-over dynamics are the dynamics of trauma: of perpetrator and victim (and sometimes hero). People become traumatized when they feel victimized, when they feel powerless to control a situation in which they are under threat physically or emotionally.[29] People can also become traumatized when they witness a traumatic event and feel powerless to control the outcome. Trauma causes us to lose connection with ourselves and others; traumatized individuals feel disconnected internally and externally.[30] Traumatic events also cause and reflect shame and grandiosity. Victims often experience shame, while perpetrators are frequently in a state of grandiosity, and each role and feeling feeds the other.

Power-over dynamics are also the dynamics of addiction. An addicted person is in a state of powerlessness, or disempowerment. They are also victimized by the addiction; the object of their addiction has total power and control over them, and often the experience of addiction is traumatic for them, and usually for others in their life as well.

Two drivers of addiction are a feeling of disconnection and a sense of disempowerment. Addictive behaviors create a temporary feeling of connection (i.e., a "oneness" or "unity" within oneself and with others) and empowerment. However, once the high (from drinking, gambling, sex, etc.) wears off, the feelings of disconnection and disempowerment often actually increase.

People who suffer from addiction also experience both shame and grandiosity. On one level, they often feel profound shame for their sense of powerlessness to control their own behaviors. At the same time, their "inner addict," the part of their psyche that drives them to maintain the addiction, may believe that they are in control of something they actually have no control over, so they perceive themselves as more powerful than they actually are.

Trauma and addiction are two sides of the power-over coin; they are both expressions of power-over dynamics, and they tend to reinforce one another. It is no coincidence that many people who have been traumatized also suffer from addiction, and that addiction is often a traumatizing experience for the individual who is addicted (as well as for those in their life).

Power-with dynamics, by contrast, are the dynamics of love and, ultimately, of mindfulness, of presence. Presence is essentially the opposite of trauma and addiction. Presence is a state of mindfulness—of connection and nonviolence, whereas trauma results from and causes disconnection and violence. And although addiction creates a *sense* of connection—making us feel, temporarily, unified with others and ourselves—it is ultimately disconnecting. Moreover, presence is also a state of acceptance and awareness, whereas addiction is a state of craving that relies on self-delusion for its fulfillment. When we are in a state of addiction, we are focused on one thing: gratification of the addictive "fix," be it alcohol, working, or our own self-perception. And we may use any means necessary toward this end, even if such means involve violating our integrity (which they often do). When we are in a state of presence, however, we are not attached to an identity or ego or to an outcome that we try to control, so we are able to be open to, and connected with, what are perhaps the deepest aspects of ourselves and others: our shared mortality and dignity. We are able to express and receive love in perhaps the truest sense of the word.

• • •

With an understanding of power models and dynamics, we can turn our attention to the second condition necessary for oppression: a system. Together, power-over dynamics and a system create the oppressive system of powerarchy.

CHAPTER 3

Systems of Power

It is no measure of health to be well adjusted to a profoundly sick society.

–JIDDU KRISHNAMURTI (ATTRIBUTED)

n 1633, the renowned mathematician Galileo Galilei was convicted of heresy. He was placed under house arrest for the rest of his life, and it was forbidden that he or others publish any of his future works. His crime? Supporting the theory of his predecessor Copernicus, who'd argued that the planets revolved around the sun. The prevailing belief was that the planets revolved around the earth; the earth was the exalted center of the universe. To proclaim otherwise, even when such an assertion was supported by sound mathematical calculations, was not only to call into question the validity of established scientific and religious assumptions but also to expose the fact that such assumptions were based on a dogmatic and irrational belief system. Such a system is unable to stand up to scrutiny, so it depends on its proponents to deny, condemn, and even kill in order to maintain its status quo.

Social scientists have long since demonstrated the power of systems, including entrenched belief systems, to influence human psychology and social behavior. However, widespread ignorance and denial of the impact of systems persist, which is a key reason why oppressive dynamics continue unchecked. Were we to truly appreciate how systems shape our lives and world, we would be better able to challenge those systems that turn random or isolated power-over behaviors into widespread, institutionalized oppression.

Indeed, although power-over dynamics inform oppression, for oppression to manifest fully, power-over dynamics need a vehicle, a structure or framework through which they may be more fully incorporated into a relationship or society. Power over, in other words, needs a system to house and disseminate it. It is the synthesis of power-over dynamics with a system to codify and legitimize them that gives rise to powerarchy.

SYSTEMS: THE DANCES THAT SHAPE OUR LIVES AND OUR WORLD

A **system** is a set of interconnected parts that form a whole, which, as systems psychologist Harriet Lerner points out, is similar to a dance.[1] A dance is made up of dancers, music, and dance steps, and the way these parts come together creates the whole integrated ensemble. In some dances, we may feel insecure and self-conscious; in others, we may feel confident and inspired. In some dances, we may have our toes stepped on and be forced to follow the other's lead, even if we don't want to; in others, we may move gracefully together, as true partners.

Some systems include just one other person, as with a couple system, whereas some include millions of others, as with social systems. When only two people are involved in a system, we usually refer to it simply as a "relationship." Larger systems are, essentially, sets of relationships. We even have an internal system: according to a new psychological model, our personality is not one cohesive whole but comprises multiple parts, or personalities, that are always interacting with one another, for better or worse.[2]

Like dances, each system has its own personality. The personality of a system is made up of the personalities and behaviors of the people in it, as well as the way these individuals interact or come together. A family, for example, is more than just the composite of its members. The way that all those members interact creates the particular personality of the family as a whole. Families can be fun-loving and spontaneous, serious and deliberate, supportive and loving, abusive and dysfunctional, and so on.

The parts of a system include people (or in some cases, nonhuman animals or nature) who play certain **roles**, and **rules**, or guidelines, that dictate how the people should behave and experience themselves (and others) in their roles. Any role or rule in a given system can be *explicit,* stated aloud or otherwise consciously acknowledged, or *implicit,* unstated and therefore often unconscious.

Although many roles we play in our systems are explicit—such as father, sister, manager, or chairperson—most are implicit. For example, in our personal relationships, we may be the "underfunctioner" when we struggle to maintain our responsibilities, or the "overfunctioner" when we take on the responsibilities of the other person, who is underfunctioning. Or on the social stage, we may be the "rational, impartial moderate" when we speak on behalf of an established social system, or the "emotional, biased radical" when we challenge that system.

As with roles, some rules are explicit, such as "no swearing in the house" or "no sexual relations outside the marriage," but most are implicit, such as "nobody talks about Dad's drinking." Other implicit rules might be that the overfunctioner makes the important decisions for the couple or that the person challenging the established social system is not to be taken seriously.

Many of the most powerful systems in our lives are those whose roles and rules we've never overtly learned, but that we've unconsciously and fully integrated into our experience. We step to songs we don't hear with partners we don't see, keeping alive dances we might otherwise choose to end. For example, we may be well into our middle years before we realize that we've been playing the role of "caretaker" our entire life—that many of our relationships have been with people who have needed us to take care of their needs to the detriment of our own. Or it may be only after our adult child comes out as gay that we realize we've been perpetuating prejudice and discrimination through our attitudes and behaviors.

Social scientists have noted two key types of systems—open and closed. An **open system** is open to change and a **closed system** is closed, or resistant, to change. Of course, like most phenomena, systems exist on a spectrum, so a system can be more or less open or closed.

In an open system, roles can change, and rules are fluid. Roles and expectations shift as situations change and/or members of the system grow. For example, in a family system, if the provider loses their job, rather than colluding in judgment and shame, the family responds supportively, with compassionate and reflective understanding and perhaps by rearranging the family structure so that another person willingly takes on the role of provider. Or when a person in a wheelchair points out that the design of their workplace doesn't meet their needs, they are heard, validated, and attended to rather than framed as controlling—as trying to impose their needs on others.

In a closed system, roles and rules are rigid and unchanging. Closed systems seek to maintain the status quo, the way things are, even if everyone involved is miserable. Most of us have known couples who are spectacularly unhappy in their relationship, yet each partner has a long list of reasons why any change would be impossible. Closed systems force conformity: either we conform to the roles and rules of the system, or we are forced out. If, for example, everyone at the company we're employed by chronically overworks and we also overwork, we'll be accepted and celebrated. If we choose not to conform to this expectation, chances are high that we'll be seen as uncommitted and that we'll end up either being fired or wanting to quit.

Sometimes, closed systems appear to be changing when in fact they are not—they're just reconfiguring themselves. For example, in a couple relationship, when the person playing the role of "distancer of intimacy" changes their tune and starts pursuing greater closeness, the other person, who has been playing the role of "pursuer of intimacy," may suddenly get cold feet and start distancing (which often makes the pursuer pursue even more). So the pursuer-distancer system doesn't really change at all: the partners simply swap roles, and the original dynamic and level of intimacy stay in place.[3] Or when members of disadvantaged social groups—groups with less social power—are finally granted access to more power, they may find that such access is largely fraudulent. For instance, the "sexual revolution" of the 1970s enabled women to break out of their traditional gender role, which had placed their value almost entirely on their ability to provide for men in the domestic arena and which limited their freedom of sexual expression. However, with their newfound sexual liberation came the expectation not that they would stop being domestic providers for the men with whom they were partnered but that they would also be sexual providers. So women became domestically and sexually objectified.[4] Neither situation honored women as inherently worthy or truly afforded them the opportunity to grow beyond roles that served to maintain the patriarchal status quo.

Perhaps not surprisingly, open systems tend to be organized around the power-with model, and closed systems tend to be organized around the power-over model. And power-over systems are those to which I refer as powerarchies.

POWERARCHY

A powerarchy is a system that reflects and reinforces the power-over model, and which is organized around the belief in a hierarchy of moral worth. A powerarchy has an unjust imbalance of power among the groups or individuals in it, and it's structured in such a way as to maintain and often grow this power imbalance. Indeed, the whole structure of powerarchies ensures that power never balances out. (Systems that simply have an imbalance of power and are not based on a hierarchy of moral worth, such as that of a parent and a child, are not necessarily powerarchies.) By contrast, power-with systems, which are organized around integrity, may become increasingly balanced in the distribution of power as they evolve.

A continual increase in a power imbalance is often a hallmark of any system in which one individual or group exercises power over the other, even if the power-over dynamics are so subtle as to be undetectable. Subtle power-over dynamics can take many forms, such as indirect criticism (e.g., a woman praising her partner for joining a gym while pointing out how much better he'll feel once he's looking better); withdrawal (e.g., refusing to engage in a conversation that isn't in the interest of the **powerholder**, the individual or group with more power); internal criticism (e.g., degrading and shaming ourselves in our internal dialogue); and **projection** (e.g., creating negative stereotypes about social groups who challenge powerarchies, such as framing feminists as angry man-haters). With each repetition of the power-over dynamic, the system is bolstered and the power imbalance is maintained or increased.

As with all systems, powerarchies can be as small as two people (or smaller, if we include our internal system) or as large as millions of individuals. On the interpersonal level, powerarchies are often abusive dyadic relationships, family systems, or work cultures.[5] On the social level, powerarchies are systems of oppression.[6] These large-scale **social powerarchies** are systems such as racism, sexism, and classism, whose structure ensures that groups with social power remain in power and that power-over dynamics remain the dominant way of relating.

Social powerarchies are *dominant systems*, meaning they are so widespread that their tenets are seen as universal truths, the way things are and the way things are meant to be, rather than as a widely held set of opinions. They are invisible, woven through the fabric of society to shape norms, laws, beliefs, behaviors, and so on. Social powerarchies impact (and create) many of our deeply held beliefs, and they influence everything from whose opinions we take more seriously to whose needs we perceive as more valid and whose version of history we teach our children—some historians, for instance, have pointed out that history is truly *his* story and that a more objective and fact-based analysis of history shows a very different picture of human nature and gender than we have been led to believe.[7] And social powerarchies impact virtually all of our interactions, from those with strangers to those with whom we share our most intimate selves. However, because most of us are not conscious of the fact that we are being influenced in such a way, we unknowingly bring these powerarchical dynamics into our hearts and homes, where they can wreak havoc on our lives and relationships and where we may re-create and reinforce them even as we work to transform such systems on the societal level.

Each social powerarchy is organized around a central belief—a myth—that a particular type of individual is more worthy than another, and the system justifies such a belief by valuing the (supposed) qualities inherent in that type of individual over those in others.[8] One way to see the values associated with each social powerarchy is to look at the terminology associated with the opposing groups within it. We tell boys and men, for instance, to "man up" or to "act like a man" when we want them to "improve" themselves or their behavior. Likewise, we associate masculinity with strength (defined as the ability not to be emotional or vulnerable, characteristics seen as "feminine"), rationality, independence, and authority. Conversely, we associate women and femininity with emotionality and irrationality, dependence, and fragility. Indeed, whereas there are scant few terms that degrade girls and woman for being like boys or men (and such terms—for example, "tomboy" or "butch"—can be neutral or simply applied to women's sexual orientation and don't necessarily reflect poorly on masculinity), the most degrading terms to apply to a boy or man are those that mark him as female. For instance, we denigrate boys and men by calling them "sissies," "pussies," and "bitches," and by telling them they "throw (or run) like a girl." "Girl" and "woman," when applied to boys and men, are actually slurs. (Imagine the impact on the

psyches of girls and women when their very gender, a central feature of who they are, represents the most despised and shameful
way to be.) Similarly, we use a range of positive descriptors for
"white," such as "pure," "clean," and "good," while the opposite
holds true for "black." And we don't get punished for telling
white lies, which aren't so bad, while we get "blacklisted" if we've
done something that really is bad. Unless we are explicitly educated about social powerarchies, we simply assume that, for example, it is preferable to be rational than emotional (and to assume
that these qualities cannot coexist), that men are emotionally
stronger than women, and that boys have more value than girls.

Because the overarching myth, or *metamyth*, of all powerarchies
is the myth of a hierarchy of moral worth, one could argue that all
oppressive systems are subideologies of the *metasystem*, the overarching system of powerarchy. Powerarchy is the ethos; it is the hub of
the wheel from which all the spokes radiate.[9]

Social powerarchies are also interlocking, in that they overlap
with and reinforce one another, as noted in chapter 1.[10] Take, for
example, the concept of "successful aging," a myth that dominates
the field of (Western) gerontology, and which reflects and reinforces
not only ageism but a variety of other interlocking powerarchies.
Critics of this model point out that successful aging, which entails
retaining the qualities and features of members of younger age
groups, essentially means *not aging*—and, therefore, that there is no
inherent value of members of older age groups. They point out
that this myth sets us all up to fail, as none of us can actually not
age.[11] Moreover, the successful aging model is classist, because
in order to feel—or even "pass as"—younger, we must have the socioeconomic means to do so: we must have access to, for instance,
quality health care and nutrition. The model is ableist as well, suggesting that the development of a disability—such as needing a
wheelchair—amounts to failure.[12] And it perpetuates heterosexist
and sexist norms of, for example, virile males and attractive females
whose beauty is equated with both youth and their personal worth.[13]

In short, individual powerarchies, such as ageism and ableism, not only tailor the powerarchical metamyth that certain individuals are more worthy than others for specific demographics, such as older people or people with disabilities, but also interlock, with each myth reinforcing the others.

POWER ROLES AND RULES

Powerarchies create roles based on an unequal distribution of power, or **power roles**. In an interpersonal relationship, the powerholder may, for instance, be the "abuser," or the controlling partner. In social powerarchies, the role we play is determined by the social group or groups we belong to. Our social group is based on such factors as race, gender, social class, sexual orientation, ideology, and even species. So, for example, our role may be "white" or "black" or "brown"; "man" or "woman" or "genderqueer"; "poor" or "working class" or "upper class"; "heterosexual" or "asexual" or "homosexual"; "young" or "old"; or even "human" or "animal."[14] And, because powerarchies are interlocking, our power role can reflect multiple groups at once, such as "brown working-class woman." Social scientists refer to these social groups as "dominant" and "nondominant."[15]

Members of dominant groups have too much power, whereas members of nondominant groups have too little power, and this unbalanced distribution of power perpetuates the social powerarchy. For example, according to 2016 population estimates, people of color make up 49 percent of the US population,[16] but they constitute less than 20 percent of voting members of Congress[17] and only 19 percent of Donald Trump's presidential cabinet.[18] And research has shown that the vast majority of white Americans harbor racist attitudes, either overtly or subtly.[19] So members of the dominant, white group who hold significantly more social power than members of the nondominant, "non-white" group often support legislation and policies that inevitably reinforce racism.

Powerarchies create rules to ensure that everyone continues playing their roles so that the status quo of the system is maintained. The rules of powerarchies encourage people to do the very things that prevent power from balancing out, rendering the powerarchy self-perpetuating: the more everyone follows the rules and thus plays the roles of the powerarchy, the more they reinforce the idea that such rules are legitimate and the more fixed they all become in their roles. For example, one rule of patriarchy is that boys and men should be dominant and active and girls and women should be subordinate and passive, and studies have shown that teachers are more likely to encourage and reward dominance in boys and therefore to engender passivity in girls.[20] And the more that men and women identify with and play out the roles of "dominant male" and "submissive female," the more that traditional gender roles and power imbalances are reinforced—and the more that the tenets of patriarchy are legitimized. One of the (largely unconscious) ways in which these gender roles are played out is by women responding to men taking up space by making themselves smaller to take up less space, either physically, as when they sit with their legs crossed, or symbolically, as when they cede the floor to men in mixed-gender discussion groups or allow their domestic male partner to set the emotional tone for the relationship—when he's happy, she's happy, and when he's not, neither is she. As men take up more space, women take up less, and as women take up less space, men take up more.

Specifically, powerarchy rules reward conformity and punish deviation, and they are often expressed as *paths of least resistance*, a concept used by sociologist Allan G. Johnson to explain how dominant groups maintain social power in social powerarchies[21] (but which is applicable to all kinds of powerarchies). Paths of least resistance are ways of thinking and behaving that conform to the beliefs and values of the system and are the "easy" way to be. Going against a path of least resistance takes effort and often comes with a cost. For example, if a young man is with a group of male friends who happen to be making degrading jokes about women, it is far easier for him to laugh along with them than to call them on their behavior and risk being taunted himself. Or, in a powerarchical relationship where the rule is that only the powerholder is allowed to feel and express anger toward the other (because anger directed toward or about powerholders is a threat to the system, an issue we'll discuss further in chapter 5), both parties tend to grant the powerholder such an entitlement, though rarely is either conscious of this fact.[22] In fact, often what is stated explicitly contradicts the reality of this rule. For example, consider the following scenario between an abusive mother and her teenage son. The mother asks her son, who seems unhappy, what's wrong, encouraging him to open up and share what's bothering him. The son admits that since his mother started a new job and has been coming home late at night, he hasn't been sleeping well and he's feeling frustrated with her for not being quieter. The mother becomes offended and defensively attacks him, arguing that he's too light of a sleeper. Or she withdraws to sulk in self-pity, telling her son he doesn't appreciate how hard she works and how much she sacrifices for him, and guilting him into apologizing and retracting his statement. When a nonpowerholder expresses anger at a powerholder, it's sometimes a request that the powerholder change a power-over behavior, and such a request tends to be met with resistance and attempts to maintain the powerarchical norm.

THE THREE DEFENSES OF POWERARCHIES

Powerarchies—both social and interpersonal—are organized around a set of falsehoods, or **myths**,[23] that reflect the opinions of those with more power in the system but that just about everyone buys into. The myths of powerarchies are expressed through **cognitive distortions**,[24] such as denial and justification, and **narratives**, which are stories that reflect the cognitive distortions and are woven together to create an even stronger defensive structure. The myths are sustained on a practical level through **privileges** that give some individuals or groups more power than others. Cognitive distortions, narratives, and privileges are the three key defenses of powerarchies, and they interact with one another to maintain the system. (The three defenses are explained in detail in chapters 4, 5, and 6.)

Moreover, the roles and rules of powerarchies reinforce the three defenses, and vice versa, in a feedback loop: the more we play the roles and follow the rules of powerarchies, the more we validate their myths (distortions and narratives) and the more we legitimize the privileges granted to those who have more power. In addition, validating myths and legitimizing privileges reinforce our identification with our roles and increase the probability that we will play by the rules of the system. For example, in a heterosexist system, the roles we play and the rules we follow feed and reinforce heterosexist myths and maintain heterosexist privilege. In many cultures, heterosexuals do not refer to themselves as such; they simply see themselves as "normal" and view people of other sexual orientations as abnormal or deviant. Particularly among heterosexual cisgender males, whose identification is derived largely by positioning themselves as masculine—as "not gay"—there has been much bullying behavior, whereby men and boys degrade other men and boys as "sissies" or otherwise not masculine enough. Such behavior communicates that being female/feminine or transgender or otherwise gender nonconforming is an inferior and shameful—less valid— way of being. Moreover, the rules of a heterosexist system, which may deny same-sex couples the right to marry or to visit a loved one in a hospital, reinforce the myths that heterosexuality is normal, natural, and necessary and that those who are heterosexual are more worthy of moral consideration. Each time we play our roles and follow the rules of a powerarchy, we further normalize and legitimize the system.

•••

We have discussed the basic structure and nature of powerarchies. However, to truly understand and challenge these systems, we need to deconstruct them. More specifically, we must understand the three defenses that keep them propped up. In the next chapter, we will look at one defense, cognitive distortions, and examine how these distortions help maintain the unjust power imbalances of powerarchies.

CHAPTER 4

Distortions and Power

All of us show bias when it comes to what information we take in.
We typically focus on anything that agrees with the outcome we want.
–NOREENA HERTZ

I n the cult classic movie *The Matrix*, the characters believe themselves to be living normal lives, when in fact they are hooked up
to machines that have imprisoned their minds and the minds of
almost all humans. All they see, feel, and perceive is a simulated
reality, created in order to prevent them from rebelling against the
machines that are using their body heat as an energy source. It's only
when the characters are able to unplug themselves from the Matrix
that they can free their minds and see reality as it truly is. And when
they reclaim their freedom of thought, they also reclaim their freedom of choice. They no longer passively serve the violent interests
of a more powerful group of others, but instead choose to act in
accordance with their personal values and integrity. They refuse to
support an oppressive system, and they fight for justice and freedom for all of humanity.[1]

Not unlike the Matrix, powerarchies coerce (and sometimes
force) people into following the dictates of oppressive systems they
don't even know exist, into acting against their core moral values.
Most people, however, need to feel that they are living in accordance with such values, that they are living a moral life.[2] Indeed,
acting against our values causes us to feel a moral discomfort, a conscious or unconscious feeling of guilt, which can cause a form of

cognitive dissonance.[3] In order to alleviate this dissonance, we can change our values, change our behaviors (e.g., stop playing our roles and following the rules of a powerarchy when we are in a position of power), or change our perceptions of our behaviors. Most people do the latter, and herein lies the foundation of cognitive distortions, one of the three defenses that maintain powerarchies.

The cognitive distortions of powerarchies distort our perceptions and numb our feelings so that we engage in practices we would likely otherwise find deeply offensive. These defenses are nonrelational ways of thinking and feeling, and they guide many of our behaviors. Powerarchy cognitive distortions are structured to block our awareness of the consequences of our actions and to diminish our natural empathy toward others. They disconnect us from the truth of our experience, our authentic thoughts and feelings.

The cognitive distortions of powerarchies are, as noted in chapter 3, essentially a set of myths, all of which uphold the primary myth of powerarchies: that one group (or individual) is more worthy of moral consideration than others. Each distortion acts as a distancing mechanism that disconnects us from our rationality, empathy, and, ultimately, integrity.

THE TWO-PRONGED STRATEGY
OF SOCIAL POWERARCHIES

Social powerarchies keep themselves alive by ensuring that they remain more powerful than the **countersystems**—the systems that emerge as reactions and alternatives to social powerarchies—that challenge them. For example, patriarchy must remain stronger than feminism; and **carnism**—the ideology that conditions people to eat the flesh and other products of certain animals, a subideology of speciesism—must remain stronger than veganism.[4] To this end, social powerarchies use a two-pronged defensive strategy that both strengthens the social powerarchy and weakens the countersystem.[5] This strategy causes rational, compassionate people to support irrational, harmful practices without realizing what they are doing, and to become defensive whenever they are asked to reflect on their attitudes or behaviors—or even when they simply observe someone following the norms of the countersystem.

The two-pronged strategy of social powerarchies comprises two types of cognitive distortions (explained in detail in the next sections): **primary cognitive distortions**, which validate the social powerarchy, and **secondary cognitive distortions**, which invalidate the countersystem. This double strategy maintains both a power imbalance between the two opposing systems, such as that between patriarchy and feminism, and a power imbalance between members of opposing groups within the social powerarchy itself, such as between men and women.

Primary Cognitive Distortions

Primary cognitive distortions that are used to validate social powerarchies are based on the myth that supporting a social powerarchy (e.g., maintaining white supremacy) is the right thing to do. Primary distortions legitimize the social powerarchy and distort our perceptions so that we don't recognize the beliefs and consequences of the social powerarchy as oppressive or problematic.

Denial: See No Evil, Hear No Evil, Speak No Evil
Denial is a key distortion used by social powerarchies: if we deny there's a problem in the first place, then we don't have to do anything about it. Denial is expressed largely through the social powerarchy's invisibility. One way a social powerarchy remains invisible is by remaining unnamed—at least in the early stages of the development of a countersystem. (If the social powerarchy has, in fact, been identified and named, we deny that it's as "bad as it seems.") One of the roles of a countersystem is to name the social powerarchy so that it may be recognized as the oppressive system it is and can thus be challenged. For example, if we don't name carnism, the social powerarchy that veganism challenges, then eating animals appears to be simply a given, a morally neutral behavior with no

basis in a belief system. We assume that only vegans and vegetarians follow a belief system, and we don't realize that when eating animals isn't a necessity—which is the case for many, though not all, people in the world today—then it is a choice, and choices always stem from beliefs. If we don't see the carnistic system for what it is, then we can neither question nor challenge it, and we don't even realize that we have a choice when it comes to eating animals.[6]

Social powerarchies also remain invisible by keeping their victims out of sight and therefore out of public consciousness. Again, the stage of development of the countersystem matters: if the countersystem is young, then there will be less public awareness of the victimization caused by the social powerarchy. Referring back to the example of carnism, consider how, in just one week, more farmed animals are killed than the total number of people killed in all wars throughout history,[7] and their body parts are literally everywhere we turn—yet we virtually never see any of these animals alive. Moreover, farmed animals endure an almost unimaginable fate; it is well documented that from birth through death, the vast majority of them[8] experience intense and unrelenting suffering.[9] Carnism depends on our denying the suffering of these individuals, because if we didn't, we would probably have a very hard time supporting their slaughter by continuing to eat them.

Ironically, as countersystems reach maturation, they can again struggle to expose the victimization of the social powerarchy, because the violence of the system may have become more subtle, even though it may be no less damaging. For example, in the early days of the US civil rights movement, there was extreme resistance to the idea that people of color were victims of a racist system, even though the racism was blatant. Today, although many Americans accept that racism is a reality, there is also a narrative that the United States is a "postracial" society, making it a challenge to highlight the continued violence directed toward people of color. Consider the case of Trayvon Martin, a black, unarmed seventeen-year-old who was visiting relatives in a gated community in Florida when he was fatally shot by George Zimmerman, the white/Latinx twenty-eight-year-old neighborhood watch coordinator, who had assumed that Martin was trespassing to burglarize the neighborhood. Zimmerman was tried and acquitted on self-defense grounds, despite the fact that there was no hard evidence that Martin had posed a threat to Zimmerman (or anyone else).[10] The Martin case is but one of an epidemic of racialized killings in the US,[11] killings whose racial nature is denied, thus masking the continued victimization of people of color.[12]

Of course, the central myth that denial tells is that there is no social powerarchy in the first place, and therefore there is no unjust power imbalance. As with all social powerarchy myths, this myth exists both on a macro level ("powerarchies don't exist") and on a more specific level ("sexism/ageism/ableism doesn't exist").

The Three Ns of Justification: Power Over Is Normal,
Natural, and Necessary
Another cognitive distortion used by social powerarchies is *justification*. We learn to justify social powerarchies and power over in general by learning to believe in the three Ns of justification: power over (and, specifically, the power-over core belief of a particular system, such as white supremacy) is *normal, natural,* and *necessary.* These justifications are myths that are presented as facts, and they have been used to justify oppressive practices throughout the course of human history.

POWER OVER IS NORMAL   Social norms are codes of conduct, ways of being and behaving, that are considered socially acceptable and legitimate. Social norms encourage conformity: when we go along with them, our lives are easier, and we are considered normal. For example, if we are cisgender and gender conforming,[13] we'll have no (or little) problem finding a bathroom wherever we go, and we'll be seen as just like everybody else, part of the dominant group, the "normal" people. The paths of least resistance, discussed in chapter 3, maintain the powerarchical social norm; they reward conformity to the system and punish deviation from it.

The social norms of a social powerarchy prevent us from seeing the system's irrationality: when everybody's doing something, it can be difficult to see how that "something" may make very little sense. For example, many well-intentioned people support the concept of "humane" (sometimes referred to as "organic") meat. These people are willing to spend more money in order not to support animal cruelty—they are voting with their dollar, hoping to make a positive difference in the system. However, the idea of humane animal foods becomes irrational the moment we step outside the carnistic box: most of us would consider it cruel to slaughter a happy, healthy golden retriever simply because people like the way her legs taste, yet when the very same thing is done to individuals of other species, we are told to consider it kind. Because carnism is so normal, we don't realize that "humane meat" is, in fact, a contradiction in terms.

And of course, what we call "normal" is simply the beliefs and behaviors of the dominant culture. Social norms change over time as societies evolve. For example, it was once normal and acceptable to stone women who were suspected of infidelity[14] or to refer to people in wheelchairs (and people with other kinds of disabilities) as "invalids"[15] and to construct environments that made it impossible for them to participate in social life.[16] These behaviors are now considered reprehensible, at least in many places in the world.

Cultural relativism is another way power over may be seen as normal and therefore justifiable. Cultural relativism is the belief that the values and practices of a culture should not be judged as unethical simply based on how they compare to those of other cultures. In this view, North Americans, for example, shouldn't deem eating dogs unethical when doing so is a cultural norm in other cultures.

Although it's important to consider and respect differences in cultural norms as we work to transform oppression, it's also important to recognize that cultural relativism can be used as a justification for oppression. For example, although we would obviously not want to promote racist or ethnocentric attitudes by judging people who eat dogs, at the same time, we would not want to use the fact that because in some places people eat dogs, this means that slaughtering and consuming animals is a morally neutral behavior. Many, perhaps most, social powerarchies are global, so just because one culture may have a different way of expressing and sustaining the social powerarchy does not mean that the behavior is not oppressive. In short, Asian carnism does not justify North American carnism any more than African heterosexism justifies European heterosexism. So even though the *content* of a social powerarchy may change—dogs rather than cows may be consumed, for example—the *process* of exercising power over others, the process of oppression, may remain the same.

POWER OVER IS NATURAL   Social powerarchies also justify themselves by presenting their tenets as natural, or "the way things are meant to be." This myth is maintained in large part by the disciplines of science and history.

When we look at science through the lens of a social powerarchy, we construct research that confirms the belief that one group is naturally superior to (and therefore more worthy of moral consideration than) another or others, and we legitimize unjust power imbalances and oppression. Consider, for example, the Nazi's use of craniometry and eugenics, or what feminist researcher Cordelia Fine refers to as "neurosexist" research—pseudoneuroscience that is used to demonstrate that, for example, females are biologically better at empathizing with (and thus caregiving for) others.[17]

When we look at history through the lens of a social powerarchy, what we seek and how we interpret what we discover legitimizes the social powerarchy. For example, when the Nazis looked at history through the lens of anti-Semitism, they sought—and found—evidence "proving" the "natural" inferiority of non-Aryans. Indeed, what we learn to call "natural" is often simply the dominant culture's interpretation of history.

POWER OVER IS NECESSARY   Justifying a social powerarchy as necessary is perhaps the most powerful way to sustain it. If we believe that a practice is a necessity—for the survival of a race, social order, species, and so on—then it becomes inevitable and as such exempt from ethical implications. Rather than being seen as a choice, the behavior is seen as a given. For example, if we believe that keeping our national borders closed to refugees or invading other countries that host potential threats to our own are necessary for our security, then doing so seems merely a matter of self-defense: if we don't kill others, we will die (or be harmed) ourselves. Most genocidal propaganda has relied on promoting the social powerarchy as necessary in order to garner the approval of a populace whose fear drives them to support practices that are deeply opposed to their core moral values. Consider, for instance, how the Rwandan ruling party, the Hutus, claimed that total extermination of the Tutsi opposition, which included all Tutsi "accomplices" (i.e., civilians), was an act of self-defense;[18] or Nazi minister of propaganda Joseph Goebbels's claim that Bolshevism and Jews were synonymous, and that "Bolshevism is the declaration of war by Jewish-led international subhumans against culture itself."[19] One of the key aims of social justice movements is to debunk the myth of necessity, because as soon as a behavior is recognized as a choice rather than a given, it takes on an ethical dimension it didn't previously have.

Often what we learn to think of as necessary is simply what's necessary to maintain a social powerarchy. For example, to preserve a system that privileges the very wealthy, it is indeed necessary to continue capitalist financial policies that make it difficult or impossible for those from working-class or poor communities to access the education, training, and networks they need in order to be truly "upwardly mobile."

Institutionalized Powerarchy

Social powerarchies are **institutionalized**, meaning that they are supported and promoted by all major social institutions, such as medicine, law, education, and business. In other words, the systems are woven through the structure of society, shaping norms, laws, traditions, and our very way of life. When a system is institutionalized, its beliefs and practices are promoted as facts rather than opinions and are accepted unquestioningly by the majority. For example, a strong bias against homosexuality was once institutionalized. It was classified by the medical community as a mental illness; same-sex couples were not allowed to marry; and heterosexuality was considered the normal, natural, necessary way of life for all people.

When we are born into an institutionalized system, we absorb the system's logic as our own. In other words, we internalize it.

Internalized Powerarchy

Social powerarchies use a set of cognitive distortions designed to "other" the victims of the system, causing us (when we're in a powerholding position) to perceive them as fundamentally different from, and inferior to, ourselves—as separate from us and less worthy than we are. These distortions are **objectification, deindividualization**, and **dichotomization**.

Objectification—perceiving someone as an object—can be seen in how patriarchy teaches us to view women as sexual objects for male gratification and in how ableism leads us to view people with disabilities as objects for inspiration gratification. So, for instance, men may refer to a woman as a "piece of ass," and non-disabled people may watch "inspiration porn" to get the warm fuzzies witnessing sensationalized depictions of people with disabilities purportedly overcoming adversity.[20] Deindividualization—perceiving someone as an abstraction, lacking individuality or a personality—can be seen in how ableist culture teaches us to view people who have disabilities as all alike. So we are encouraged to assume, for example, that a person who is blind but can walk shares the same experience as a person who is sighted but is in a wheelchair. And dichotomization—placing individuals into oppositional categories in our minds so that we harbor different feelings and carry out different behaviors toward members of different groups—is exemplified in the belief that Muslims are dangerous and Christians are trustworthy, or that poor or working-class teenagers smoking pot are "slackers," whereas wealthy teens doing the same are "experimenting" or "being kids."

Secondary Cognitive Distortions: Invalidating Countersystems

When enough people start to question and then challenge a social powerarchy, a countersystem is formed, which may evolve into a social justice movement. Of course, as closed systems that resist change, social powerarchies fight back. When we look back on history, we can see that many of the beliefs we accept today as rational, ethical, and essential to a functional society were dismissed, invalidated, ridiculed, and even met with violent hostility. For example, it was once considered ludicrous and offensive for people of color to patronize the same institutions as white people or for women to attend university, and those who challenged such norms were socially ostracized and sometimes imprisoned or killed.

A **backlash** is the reaction of a social powerarchy to its power being threatened; it is an attempt to regain lost power. The social powerarchy, which is based on a mythology, creates new myths (and sometimes strengthens existing ones) to prevent us from taking seriously any challenges to the system. Such myths seek to invalidate the challenging system and those who represent it. For example, as feminists have challenged the misogynistic attitudes that have driven traditional, or hostile, sexism, *benevolent sexism*—which idealizes rather than disparages women, but which nevertheless maintains gender bias and thus patriarchy—has emerged as a more modern, and insidious, form of sexism.

So despite the fact that most people's values and (often) interests are in alignment with countersystems, most people are also resistant to hearing the truth about social powerarchies. This is because social powerarchies cause people to resist the very information that would free them, psychologically and emotionally, from their coercive influence. And the powerarchies do this through using secondary cognitive distortions, which are myths that seek to invalidate countersystems and those who represent them.

Secondary distortions invalidate three aspects of a countersystem. They invalidate its social movement, its ideology, and its proponents, or advocates.[21]

Secondary distortions, like primary distortions, are internalized, shaping our perceptions without our realizing it. They shape the perceptions of the powerholders within the social powerarchy and, often, of the proponents of the countersystem. For example, both males and females alike may believe the myth that females are overly emotional. So boys and men see girls and women as less able to be objective, and girls and women, including many feminists, doubt their ability to be rational and feel ashamed of their own emotional reactions. When proponents of a countersystem have internalized the myths of secondary distortions, they can end up feeling confused, frustrated, and despairing, which limits their ability to effectively promote their cause.

Secondary Denial: Invalidating Counterideologies and Social Justice Movements
Secondary denial teaches us to deny the fact that the countersystem is a valid belief system or, in the case of young movements such as the vegan movement, that it represents a valid social justice movement. We learn, for example, to believe that veganism is simply a "trend," so we fail to recognize that the vegan movement is based on the very same principles as other social justice movements, such as promoting compassion and justice and challenging the notion that a group with more power (humans) should have the right to enact violence against a group with less power (farmed animals) to serve their own ends (producing and consuming carnistic products).

Moreover, whereas primary denial teaches us to believe that there is no social powerarchy in the first place, secondary denial teaches us to believe that (therefore) there is no power imbalance between the dominant group and the nondominant group. So we assume that the playing field is level when it comes to interactions and relationships between members of these groups, and we fail to see how the re-creation of power-over dynamics in our daily lives helps keep social powerarchies in place. For example, studies have shown that in mixed-gender interactions, men are more likely to interrupt women,[22] to speak for and about them,[23] and to condescendingly explain things to them (referred to as "mansplaining"[24]). All of these conversational dynamics mirror and bolster the patriarchal myths that men are more authoritative and are meant to be dominant. But because we have learned to deny that there's a power imbalance between men and women, when a heterosexual couple enacts such a dynamic, it's rarely noticed. If it is noticed, it's typically assumed to reflect individual personality differences rather than a gendered imbalance of power that derives from and maintains a social powerarchy.

Professionals, too, may unwittingly sustain social powerarchies when they buy into the myths of secondary denial (and other distortions). For example, despite a plethora of literature documenting that in heterosexual romantic partnerships, women are more likely to be victims of abuse than men,[25] and despite decades of feminist research unearthing the significant power imbalance between male and female domestic partners, many psychotherapists still counsel heterosexual couples as though they bring equal levels of power to the table, and fail to recognize domestic abuse (which is epidemic in the United States and many other places in the world) when it is happening.[26] Domestic violence expert Lundy Bancroft points out how countless therapists will, for example, suggest that an abusive man has an "anger management problem" or that he's just reacting to his partner "pushing his buttons" or "reminding him of his mother" rather than recognize and address the underlying problem of unbalanced power roles and male entitlement.[27]

Projection: Shooting the Messenger
Perhaps the most common secondary distortion used by social powerarchies is **projection**—projecting onto proponents of a counter-system negative and inaccurate ideas about them that invalidate

their message. Projection is a form of shooting the messenger: if we shoot the messenger, we don't have to take seriously the implications of their message.[28]

Projection is often expressed through the negative stereotyping of proponents, or advocates, of countersystems. When people believe in these stereotypes, they are not only more resistant to the information being shared by those advocates but also less likely to feel connected to the advocates themselves, with whom they may even be in close relationship. Stereotypes reduce people to one-dimensional caricatures and focus on the negative, making it difficult for us to relate to the people being stereotyped. Stereotypes also cause us to assume that all people in the stereotyped group are alike—that, for example, all lesbians are the same. We may then use one negative encounter with a lesbian LGBTQ+ advocate as an excuse to invalidate the message of all LGBTQ+ advocates. Ultimately, negative stereotypes of advocates cause us to see ourselves as being in opposition to those we might otherwise see as natural allies.

Many advocates are stereotyped as "overly emotional," a framing that easily discredits their message. Overly emotional people are, by definition, not rational, and irrational people are not worth listening to. Perhaps not surprisingly, this stereotype has been used throughout human history to discredit those who have challenged social powerarchies: the US slavery abolitionists were called "sentimentalists,"[29] and the suffragists who fought for women to have the right to vote were portrayed as hysterical.[30] And consider how the media frame black protests: the proponents are often referred to as "thugs" who are "rioting" (whereas white people engaged in the very same behaviors—but with less noble motivations, such as to cheer that their sports team won a match—are referred to as "fans" who are "celebrating").[31]

Sometimes those who oppose a social powerarchy are stereotyped as being against members of the public who represent the establishment they are challenging. For example, feminists are portrayed as anti-male (even though feminism ultimately seeks to free men and boys of the violent, dysfunctional, and nonrelational limitations patriarchy imposes on them), and LGBTQ+ advocates are often framed as "anti-family." This "anti" stereotype is based largely on the assumption that people can't be, for example, pro-female *and* pro-male, supportive of LGBTQ+ relationships *and* supportive of cisgender, heterosexual couples. In fact, the opposite is more likely to be the case: compassion begets compassion. The more compassion we allow into our lives, the more compassion we are likely to feel overall. Framing advocates as "anti" is an effective way to reduce their threat to the social powerarchy. If much of the population believes that advocates are against them, then the countermovement will surely not attract enough supporters to weaken the oppressive system it's challenging.

Another projection is that of the "omniscient" advocate, expressed through the expectation that advocates should have a fully conceptualized system ready to put in place to replace the one they are opposing. For example, those who challenge capitalism may be expected to have all the answers to the problem of the system whenever they discuss the issue, to be experts on economics, politics, philosophy, and so on.[32] And when they can't answer all the questions thrown their way (or even in the cases when they can, but their responses aren't considered legitimate), their entire ideology may come into question. It's as though someone only has a right to challenge a social powerarchy when they have all the answers to solve the problems caused by it.

In addition, advocates may be expected to live up to an impossible ideal: women are expected to climb to the top of the professional ladder, but either they have to act like men in order to do so (because "masculine" qualities, such as stoicism and assertiveness, are necessary for success in many professions) and then are criticized for being "cold" or "bitches," or they act like women, and then are stereotyped as shallow and vain, or too weak for the job.[33]

Sometimes, advocates are stereotyped as mentally ill. Pathologizing those who challenge oppressive systems isn't new: before the abolition of slavery in the United States, for example, people classified as slaves who attempted to escape were diagnosed with the mental illness "drapetomania," as it was considered crazy not to want to be enslaved.[34]

Secondary Justification

Whereas primary justification teaches us to believe that the tenets of the social powerarchy are normal, natural, and necessary, secondary justification teaches us to believe that the tenets of the counter-system are *ab*normal, *un*natural, and *un*necessary. For example, consider how this framing has been used to invalidate the LGBTQ+ movement through invalidating those representing it: until 1973, homosexuality was classified as a mental illness in the *Diagnostic and Statistical Manual of Mental Disorders*, the bible of US psychiatry.[35] Although public opinion has changed significantly since then (at least in some societies), similar anti-LGBTQ+ rhetoric nevertheless persists. Secondary justification has also been used to invalidate feminism by perpetuating the myth that granting girls and women equal social power and control is abnormal, unnatural, and unnecessary. As a result, girls and women tend to automatically cede power and control to boys and men, and the patriarchal power imbalance is maintained.

DECREASING THE POWER OF DISTORTIONS THROUGH INCREASING AWARENESS

Social transformation is not about simply eliminating a particular behavior; it is about transforming the system that gives rise to that behavior in the first place. Of course, systems and the behaviors they breed are part of a feedback loop: the more we engage in the behavior, the more we reinforce the mythology of the system, and vice versa. So social change relies on both providing incentives to change behaviors (such as making it easier to make more environmentally friendly lifestyle choices) and exposing the defenses that keep social powerarchies alive—raising awareness of the defensive structure of social powerarchies and debunking the myths they are based on.

Transforming a social powerarchy therefore requires developing an awareness of the elusive nature of social powerarchy distortions. These defenses attempt to invalidate anything—any idea, person, behavior, and so on—that challenges the system. Even some of the most rational and progressive individuals can end up defending a social powerarchy whose structure they are unaware of. For example, during the American Civil War, some moderates argued that, although slavery was wrong, enslaved people were not actually capable of taking care of themselves, so it was ultimately better for them to remain enslaved.[36] Often, logical fallacies are the result not of an inability to think logically but of the distorted thinking that emerges when a powerarchy is seeking to defend itself.

Indeed, research suggests that when people become aware of their cognitive distortions, they are less influenced by them,[37] so it stands to reason that such awareness can weaken social powerarchies. In other words, when people become aware not only of the consequences of a social powerarchy—such as the extensive non-human animal suffering and environmental degradation that results from carnism[38]—but also of the cognitive distortions of the system, they may be better able to make choices that reflect what they authentically think and feel rather than what they've been conditioned to think and feel. Only with awareness can people make their choices freely, because without awareness, there *is* no free choice.

• • •

One key reason why social powerarchy distortions are so powerful and difficult to challenge is that they are woven through the broader narratives that keep the roles and rules of the system intact. Understanding the nature and structure of narratives, then, is an essential step in transforming oppression, and it is the focus of the next chapter.

CHAPTER 5

Narratives of Power

What happens is of little significance compared with the stories we tell ourselves about what happens.

–RABIH ALAMEDDINE

I n 2008, an advertising intern inadvertently came up with what turned out to be an ingenious idea for a marketing campaign for the breakfast cereal Shreddies.[1] Shreddies were little whole-wheat squares, similar to Chex, and the campaign sought to increase the appeal (and therefore the sales) of the cereal without changing a single aspect of the product itself. The strategy? Transform public perception such that the commonplace squares became special diamonds. Thus Shreddies were reborn as Diamond Shreddies, and they boasted a market share increase of 18 percent during the first month of what became an award-winning campaign.

Although admittedly overly simplistic, the Diamond Shreddies campaign offers a poignant example of the power of storytelling. Indeed, when we look back over the course of history, we can see that it is shaped by many factors, perhaps the most powerful of which are stories. Beneath every social powerarchy and every countersystem that seeks to challenge the social powerarchy are stories that guide them: we cannot, for example, take up arms against others without first believing the story that the others are our enemies who must be conquered, just as we cannot stand together in protest against violent invasions without believing the story that the invasion is unjust.

Stories shape our world, and our lives, for better or worse. So understanding the stories of social powerarchies and how they influence our perceptions and guide our behaviors is vital to transforming oppression.

NARRATIVES

Our narrative is the story we create based on our beliefs and perceptions. Narratives can emerge from our personal experience or from our social conditioning, inherited from society. For example, if we have a personal history of being betrayed in our relationships, we may have developed a narrative that people cannot be trusted. And if we grow up in a heterosexist society, our inherited narrative may be that heterosexuality is normal and natural—and that other sexual orientations are abnormal and unnatural. Often, our narratives are a synthesis of our personal and social experience.[2]

Narratives shape our perceptions, which create our feelings. Together, our perceptions and feelings drive our behaviors. For example, if our partner left the kitchen in a mess before leaving for work in the morning and our narrative is that they just didn't care enough to pick up after themselves, we may feel angry and therefore criticize them when we see them later. However, if our narrative is instead that they were in a rush and ran out of time, we will feel and respond differently. And when the widely accepted narrative was that women were too irrational to make sound and objective decisions, people feared and distrusted women's ability to manage power, so women were not allowed to vote.[3]

Dominant narratives are the narratives of the individual or group with more power in a powerarchy. Although sometimes a dominant narrative reflects a cognitive distortion, such as the myth "male supremacy is normal," often dominant narratives are made up of several such myths woven together to create an elaborate fiction that's far more difficult to debunk than a single falsehood. Dominant narratives are like perceptual tapestries, which are greater than the sum of their parts and are much more challenging to un-ravel than an individual tangled string of yarn. And **social power-archy narratives** are the dominant narratives that mirror and bolster the mythology of the social powerarchy and that members of all groups—dominant and nondominant—grow up learning and believing.[4]

Dominant narratives constitute one of the three defenses that sustain social powerarchies (and all powerarchies). For example, both heterosexuals and nonheterosexuals learn to believe the het-erosexist social powerarchy narrative that heterosexuality is normal and natural and that other sexualities are abnormal and unnatural, or deviant, which is one reason for the high rates of suicides among LGBTQ+ teenagers.[5] Social powerarchy narratives are constructed to delude people into supporting oppression and to silence the voices of people who seek to tell the truth.

Social powerarchy narratives are perhaps the most powerful de-fense sustaining social powerarchies, and they are also the most difficult to challenge: they coerce us to do their bidding while pre-venting us from seeing the consequences of our actions and mak-ing us believe that we are operating of our own free will. Social powerarchy narratives are like living entities that take up residence in our psyches without our awareness, with a survival instinct that drives them to keep themselves alive. Unbeknownst to us, we look at the world through the eyes of a narrative that feeds on whatever validates it and rejects anything that might alert us to the fact that we've been psychologically possessed.[6]

UNBALANCED TRUST IN NARRATIVES

Social powerarchies maintain and grow their unjust power imbal-ances in large part by conditioning us to have a skewed sense of trust in the narratives of opposing groups within the powerarchies. We learn to trust social powerarchy narratives too much and the chal-lenging narratives, or **counternarratives**, too little. Our unbalanced trust in narratives is, perhaps above all else, what keeps social powerarchies, and all powerarchies, intact. Whether on the broadest social level or the most intimate, interpersonal level, our tendency to trust narratives either too much or too little is the lifeblood of these systems.

In powerarchies, those with less power are more likely to see themselves through the eyes of those with more power—and to believe the dominant narrative—than vice versa. Whenever there's a power differential, this is the case: consider, for example, how much more impact saying "You're stupid" has when said by a parent to a child than the other way around. This is one reason why the very people who would normally oppose a social powerarchy can end up supporting it. For example, LGBTQ+ teenagers living in a heterosexist social powerarchy often believe that something is wrong with them, even when their own narrative and associated feelings are perfectly natural for them. And many girls and women believe that their primary value comes from being physically attractive to boys and men, even though they know, on some level, that their value is much deeper. Moreover, studies have found that older people tend to perceive themselves as—and therefore act—less physically and sexually vital than they actually are, having bought into the narratives of an ageist powerarchy.[7]

DEFINING REALITY: THE MASS HYPNOSIS OF SOCIAL POWERARCHIES

Defining reality is dictating the truth of another's experience— appointing oneself the expert on what another is thinking or feeling, even when they say otherwise.[8] For example, perhaps a boy falls and scrapes his knee and starts crying, only to be told that the cut "isn't that bad" and therefore that "there's no reason to be upset." The boy learns to distrust the signals his body and feelings are giving him, and as similar experiences build up over the years, he grows into a man who has to be on his deathbed before he'll see a doctor and who finds it nearly impossible to identify and articulate his emotions. And the dominant white culture argues that racism no longer exists, despite the repeated commentary of people of color whose personal experience directly contradicts such a claim.[9] On the intrapersonal level, we can define our own reality—for example, we may say to ourselves that we "shouldn't" be feeling depressed because what we're experiencing "isn't such a big deal."

Defining reality is problematic no matter who does it or why it is done, because the process is fundamentally invalidating. Defining reality communicates that another's experience—and, by extension, their self—is invalid. To be invalid is to be wrong or to be worthless. So defining reality is inherently shaming; it is disempowering and disconnecting and it is an act of power over.

Defining reality is the foundation of psychological abuse, and it is an essential weapon in the arsenal of cult leaders, domestic abusers, totalitarian regimes, and anyone who seeks power and control over others. Defining reality causes others to lose trust in their thoughts and feelings, thus eroding their self-confidence and stripping them of their sense of empowerment and agency. In its extreme form, defining reality is "gaslighting"—intentionally getting others to distrust their experience such that they lose the ability to know what's real and they therefore turn all power and control over to others. Consider, for example, how President Trump has repeatedly stated that the news media—meant to act as the eyes and ears of the public—is not to be trusted,[10] and how public trust in the media has plummeted.[11]

The more a powerholder (or powerholding group) defines another's (or others') reality, the more the other believes the powerholder's version of reality over their own, and therefore the more they shape their lives to appease the needs and wants of the powerholder. For example, in abusive relationships, the victim often ends up making excuses for the abuser's behavior ("He's just going through a stressful period," or "I'm not that easy to live with either"); assuming responsibility for the abuse ("I shouldn't have been so critical; then she wouldn't have gotten so mad at me"); overfocusing on the needs of the abuser; and neglecting themselves so that their perceptions and world revolve around the abuser. And often, the abuser isolates the victim, cutting them off from outside voices that would challenge the abuser's version of reality. A similar dynamic can be seen on the social level. For example, the lack of accurate representations of Asian Americans in popular US culture reinforces shallow stereotypes of members of this group—the high-achieving math student, the martial artist, or the sexualized geisha—while the overrepresentation of white people reinforces whiteness as the norm and the cultural ideal. This narrative defines the reality of Asian Americans (and many people of color). Asian Americans often end up conforming to the white norm and adapting in order to meet the needs of white people, who occupy most positions of power and are the primary cultural decision-makers.

Whenever we impose our narrative on others, we are defining their reality—and social powerarchy narratives are imposed on everyone, creating a sort of mass hypnosis. The oppressive narratives of social powerarchies are woven through our world and our lives to create a web of myths in which we're all ensnared but which virtually none of us can see.

WHEN NARRATIVES CLASH

Confirmation bias is the tendency for people to seek, notice, and remember only information that supports their existing assumptions—that confirms their narrative.[12] If, for example, we believe that humans are fundamentally good, we'll tend to notice all the examples of how helpful and kind people are and we'll tend to not see, or to explain away, or to forget, evidence that disproves our beliefs. And if we live in a culture that shares our narrative, our cognitive biases will be that much stronger: the more people there are who support a narrative, the more entrenched it becomes.

Because of the near-universal acceptance of dominant narratives as truths rather than beliefs and thus as facts rather than opinions, the dominant confirmation bias and its inevitable inaccuracies remain invisible. For this reason, dominant narratives aren't held to the same standards of accountability that counternarratives are: when nearly everyone agrees on something, they are unlikely to feel the need to examine it to ensure that it's actually accurate. For example, because just about everyone in the medical community in the fourteenth century believed in alchemy, the practice of transmuting metals to treat disease, alchemists were not held accountable for their methodology; they were not expected to prove that it was sound. And when alchemy did begin to come under scrutiny, the burden of proof lay with those representing the nondominant method, chemistry.[13]

In social powerarchies, when dominant and nondominant narratives clash or compete, the dominant narrative, which is less accountable, is nevertheless more believable to the majority. For example, when people of color describe their experiences of being on the receiving end of racist power-over dynamics, white people often argue that such commentary is a distortion or exaggeration of facts, and the dominant white narrative is more readily believed. But given that the social powerarchy of racism is so deeply entrenched that it impacts virtually all racial interactions—whether we are aware of this fact or not—and given that the dominant white narrative (and white privilege, an issue we'll discuss in the following chapter) prevents white people from recognizing the experience of people of color and causes them to define the reality of people of color, it is far more likely that a person of color's account of their experience of racism is accurate and a white person's perceptions are not.

Furthermore, because those with less power tend to distrust their own narrative and to (consciously or unconsciously) believe that of the dominant group, they tend to feel less confident and often even intimidated when narratives clash, which often prevents them from speaking out. So when a member of a nondominant group does challenge a dominant narrative, chances are they have more than ample reason to do so.

THE SOCIAL POWERARCHY METANARRATIVE AND SHAME

As noted throughout this book, the *metanarrative*, or overarching narrative, of social powerarchies (and all powerarchies) is that there is a hierarchy of moral worth, that certain groups are more worthy of moral consideration than others. Specific social powerarchy narratives reinforce this metanarrative, largely through communicating that the experiences, thoughts and opinions, feelings, and needs of powerholders are more valid than those of others. For example, when (white) Americans express their anger about immigrants (of color) "taking their jobs," the rest of society is expected to feel more concerned about their experience—to empathize more with them—than about that of the immigrants, who are, as residents or citizens, equally entitled to such jobs.

Because they are invalidating, social powerarchy narratives are typically shaming. As we discussed in chapter 2, shaming members of nondominant groups serves to maintain social powerarchies: people who feel ashamed lack the confidence and motivation that would inspire them to recognize and challenge an unfair system, to take positive action on their own (or sometimes others') behalf. (Shaming those with less power helps maintain all powerarchies, so some of the narratives explained in this section apply to interpersonal powerarchies as well.)

There are countless social powerarchy narratives, which impact the perceptions of members of both dominant and nondominant groups in a variety of ways. Some of the most notable ways our perceptions are impacted by such narratives are that

we perceive members of nondominant groups as deficient,

our perceptions of needs and control are distorted,

we perceive members of dominant groups as more authoritative,

our perceptions of the anger of members of nondominant groups are distorted, and prejudicial attitudes toward members of nondominant groups are reinforced.

Narratives and Deficiency

Social powerarchy narratives often depict members of nondominant groups as deficient.[14] Because dominant groups represent the standard for everyone and are held up as the ideal, members of nondominant groups are, by comparison, perceived as less-than (less attractive than, less competent than, less "cultured" than, etc.). For example, in ableist culture, individuals are labeled "disabled" when they have a physical or mental condition that prevents them from functioning in some particular way or ways that conform to normative expectations. Not only does the term *disabled* frame these individuals as deficient, as it focuses on the fact that they are *not* able—that they are lacking an ability—but it can also end up defining their identity in the eyes of others (and of themselves, if they're not aware of the influence of the ableist narrative), because the "disability" can become a central feature of how they are perceived. Moreover, the very concept of "disabled" reflects an arbitrary categorization. We ascribe this label to, for example, an emotionally intelligent individual who is missing an arm but not to someone who is self-centered and exploitative but who has both arms intact. Which of these individuals needs more special treatment and accommodation? For which of them must society, and other individuals, pay a higher price? (With an awareness of the limitations of current language, I have done my best to use respectful terminology. I use the term *disability* only when necessary and, whenever appropriate, with person-centered language [saying "a person who has a disability" rather than "a disabled person"].)

Narratives, Needs, and Perceptions of Control

Although a variety of factors, such as our temperament and personal history, affect how we relate to our own and others' needs, social powerarchy narratives play an important role. Social powerarchies teach us to view our needs as too important when we have more power than another, or as not important enough when we have less power than another. When we view our needs as too important, we feel a sense of entitlement. **Entitlement** is having a double standard, believing that we are deserving of special treatment: the rules that we expect others to follow don't apply to us. For example, a domestic abuser may expect his partner to listen and respond to him when he's upset about something she did, but when she asks for the same, he feels unfairly put upon—and he feels angry, as anger is the emotional response to (perceived or actual) injustice. Similarly, although in some parts of the United States the population of native Spanish speakers outnumbers that of native English speakers, many native English speakers feel resentful for having to view public signs that are bilingual.[15]

When we view our needs as too important, we also tend to view others' requests to have their needs met not as neutral requests but as unfair demands. We can therefore feel controlled—even when we're not—and react accordingly. So members of dominant groups may become righteously angry when their needs aren't met and can feel defensive when they are asked to meet the needs of members of nondominant groups. For example, research has shown that even when both spouses work full-time, women do 70–80 percent of the domestic work, including child care. And when women ask for a more equitable division of labor, men perceive such requests as unfair demands.[16]

Moreover, because members of nondominant groups have learned to devalue and dismiss their own needs, they can have trouble even recognizing them. If, for example, a woman believes that her male partner's need to feel free and uncontrolled is more important than her need to feel secure and respected, she may tell herself she's just overreacting when he does things such as flirt with other people. And even if members of nondominant groups do recognize a need of their own, they may have trouble articulating it because they sense that the other may respond with anger and because they believe in the narrative that they're making unfair demands. Furthermore, if they do articulate their need, they can end up feeling guilty and ashamed, believing that what they're asking for is invalid and unjust. Consider, for instance, how ensuring that a person with a disability is able to simply function (e.g., providing a ramp for a wheelchair to get up stairs) is typically seen as "accommodating" and often as an inconvenience rather than as honoring a basic human right.

When the needs of members of nondominant groups are seen as controlling demands, even seemingly benign needs that have no bearing or impact on the needs of members of dominant groups can be perceived as impositions. Because of the carnistic narrative, for example, parents who raise their children as vegan are often accused of "imposing their veganism on their children," whereas nonvegans are never seen as "imposing their carnism on their children." The social powerarchy of carnism also prevents us from appreciating the fact that parents naturally raise their children according to their own beliefs, which is why we don't expect Christians to raise their children as atheists or Democrats to raise their children as Republicans. (I am referring to vegans as members of a nondominant ideological group who, because of this status, are sometimes on the lower end of powerarchical dynamics. I do not mean to suggest that vegans as a group experience the same kind of oppression as do, for instance, people of color, those who are genderqueer, or those who have certain disabilities.)

Narratives and Authority

A central tenet of social powerarchies is **authoritarianism**—the belief that power should be concentrated in the hands of those deemed appropriate to exercise authority over others and that such authority is more valuable than individual freedoms. Of course, this tenet is typically not explicitly stated. It's even sometimes ostensibly opposed by the social powerarchy, as in the case of capitalism, a system that creates a centralization of power even as it claims to support democratization and decentralization of power.[17] To maintain themselves, social powerarchies need to promote authoritarianism. People who have been conditioned to trust powerholders' opinions over their own are more likely to defer to the objectives of those invested in maintaining a social powerarchy and are less likely to question or challenge the system.

These "authoritarian narratives" cause us to believe that the opinions of members of dominant groups hold more weight than do the opinions of members of nondominant groups—and if there is a difference of opinion, to place the burden of proof on the latter. Indeed, powerholders tend to see themselves as more informed than they actually are, and to perceive their opinions as facts and perceive the facts shared by members of nondominant groups as opinions. This is partly why potentially productive conversations about oppression end up as destructive debates. Opinions are subjective and open for debate, whereas facts are objective and therefore not disputable. For example, a gender-nonconforming person is generally much more informed about issues of gender than is the average cisgender heterosexual. Yet if the topic of gender arises between members of these different groups, the cisgender heterosexual person may argue passionately about issues they don't truly understand and insist that the gender-nonconforming person is wrong about the main ideas and practices of their own lifestyle, believing that the other—rather than themselves—should have to prove the validity of their position, while resisting the facts the other is sharing.

Moreover, studies have shown that when people are in positions of authority, they actually feel less empathy for others and are more likely to rely on stereotypes and generalizations when making judgments about them.[18] So they tend to be less open to narratives that challenge their authority. This mentality, of course, helps to maintain authoritarian narratives.

Narratives and Anger

Social powerarchy narratives distort perceptions of anger. Because anger, which is the emotion that arises as a reaction to unjust attitudes and behaviors, drives people to challenge injustice, it is a threat to systems that are based on injustice. If enough people within a social powerarchy are in touch with and able to express their anger about the unjust system, the powerarchy becomes destabilized.

When someone who challenges a social powerarchy expresses anger, their anger is often perceived as more intense than it actually is. Furthermore, they are often framed as "an angry person," rather than as "a person who is angry"; the focus is on a supposed internal problem with the individual rather than on the external circumstances they are angry about. For example, when women discuss sexism, the slightest hint of anger is often seen as an aggressive attack, and the women are labeled "bitches" or worse, making their anger seem as though it's a problematic aspect of their character rather than a legitimate emotional response to the injustice of patriarchy.[19] And the all-too-common label "angry black woman" demonstrates how such a stereotype is compounded by race.

Narratives and Prejudice

Social powerarchies rely on narratives that reflect and bolster prejudice. As countersystems evolve, these narratives are identified and challenged and thus are more visible. For example, although anti-Semitism is still very much a problem today and is even on the rise in certain places in the world,[20] in at least some places this prejudice has been named and challenged, so mocking a Jewish person for not eating pork, for example, is no longer tolerated in many circles. But when a countersystem is young, social powerarchy narratives can remain hidden and wreak havoc. For instance, prejudice against vegans, whose ideological minority status is largely unrecognized because veganism is still an emerging countersystem, is almost entirely invisible. Hostile humor directed against members of this group—mocking vegans for not eating animals and attacking their values and character, often in front of others—is commonplace and considered socially acceptable, as it is not recognized as the prejudicial behavior it is.

INTERNALIZED OPPRESSION AND INTERNALIZED PRIVILEGE

Internalized oppression is the phenomenon whereby those with less power in a powerarchy believe in their inferiority and act in ways that mirror and reinforce this belief. Often, this means they have bought into the negative narratives they've heard about themselves.[21] Internalized oppression causes the oppressed individual or group to act against their own interests. They help do the oppressor's job for them by participating in their own oppression and often in the oppression of others within their group. For example, many women internalize the sexist narrative that their primary value comes from being sexually attractive to men, and they end up competing with one another for male attention rather than uniting to transform the powerarchy that causes them to believe they are only as worthy as they are (heterosexually) attractive in the first place.

The flip side of internalized oppression is **internalized privilege**. Internalized privilege is the phenomenon whereby dominant individuals or groups in a powerarchy believe in their superiority and as such feel entitled to special treatment that is withheld from others, and they act accordingly. Internalized oppression and privilege create a narrative cocktail that acts as a social narcotic, inebriating us so that we continue to play our roles in, and follow the rules of, powerarchies without realizing what we're doing. (The next chapter explores the concept of privilege more fully.)

SOCIAL POWERARCHIES AND THE TRAUMA NARRATIVE

Atrocities are the inevitable end result of unchecked social powerarchies, the ultimate expression of oppressive systems. Even if the violence of a social powerarchy is, in one part of the world, "only" manifested in discriminatory and unfair treatment, elsewhere the social powerarchy may be genocidal. For example, anti-Semitism was (and is) a global system of oppression, which found its geno-cidal expression in Nazi Germany.

Atrocities are mass traumatic phenomena, and as such, they often cause both victims and witnesses of the atrocity to become traumatized. The victims range from children and their parents who have been separated at the US-Mexican border to Muslims whose communities have been bombed by invaders. The witnesses are often those who are active in countersystems (who may or may not have been victims of the social powerarchy). As advocates for the victims, the witnesses are proponents of a social cause or justice movement designed to end the violence of the social powerarchy, such as doctors on humanitarian missions in war zones, social workers who run shelters for domestic abuse survivors, and animal rights advocates who view (or capture) graphic imagery of violence toward nonhuman animals.

People who have been exposed to an atrocity can develop a worldview that is based on trauma, a **trauma narrative**, whereby they see the world as one ongoing traumatic event with only three roles to be played: victim, perpetrator, and hero. The more trau-matized the person becomes, the more rigidly they may compart-mentalize these roles, with little room left for nuance. Advocates who fight among themselves are sometimes acting out their trauma narrative. Unable to accept that good people participate in harmful practices, they assume that if someone is not acting perfectly in accordance with the ideology of the countersystem, then that per-son is a perpetrator. In other words, if someone is not a victim, then they're either a perpetrator or a hero—and heroes must be all good, all the time.

The trauma narrative is often part of a posttraumatic stress syn-drome, in which thoughts, emotions, and physical experiences become distorted and dysregulated. People who suffer from post-traumatic stress and are looking at the world through the trauma narrative can end up increasing their own traumatization. For ex-ample, they may end up developing addictions in an attempt to regulate their emotions, which makes them even less resilient to withstanding the stress they are experiencing. They may also increase the traumatization of others by, for example, guilting and shaming others whom they see as perpetrators, thus ultimately becoming that which they are fighting against.

Of course, it's important that people not use the fact that advocates can develop a posttraumatic response to witnessing atrocities as an excuse to pathologize or otherwise dismiss them. Many advocates experience minimal traumatization and are able to manage their experience without contributing to problematic relational dynamics. Moreover, advocates are doing the largely thankless and invisible work of cleaning up the mess created by others, and blaming them for having a natural psychological response to such an experience is like blaming someone who's mopping a floor on which others dumped waste for getting dirty in the process. The purpose of illuminating the trauma narrative is to help thwart the re-creation of power-over dynamics within the very systems that are designed to transform them.

DECREASING THE POWER OF NARRATIVES THROUGH INCREASING AWARENESS

Human beings are meaning-making animals, driven by narratives and destined to continue creating them. So we are always operating in the midst of narratives: to step outside of one narrative, we must already have adopted a different one.

Challenging powerarchical narratives, then, requires replacing them with alternative stories. But how do we determine which narratives to believe in? How do we distinguish fiction from fact?

The first step is to change the way we relate to narratives in general—both to dominant narratives and to our personal ones. This means maintaining an ongoing awareness of the existence of narratives in the first place, so that we don't automatically buy into them. It also means being committed to critically examining narratives: when we hear (or create) a story, we ask what facts it's based on, and how we can trust that such facts are accurate. Are, for instance, the facts produced by a reputable source, which includes the fact that the source is not invested in maintaining or growing a power imbalance? Changing the way we relate to narratives also means looking for alternative explanations for what we may accept as "truth," to try to disprove the assumptions driving the narrative, and—particularly when we're in a disadvantaged position—examining our internal experience to see how we're affected by the narrative. For example, does the narrative cause us to feel shame? When the narrative is about our own experience, does it clash with our own self-perceptions, our own understanding of ourselves and, perhaps, our group?

Perhaps most notably, we need to assess whether a given narrative is, ultimately, nonrelational or relational. Does it serve to increase or rectify a power imbalance? Does it reflect integrity and honor dignity? Or does it tell the story of moral superiority and inferiority? Of course, even when a narrative is relational, this doesn't guarantee its accuracy. However, when a narrative is nonrelational, its *in*accuracy is pretty much a given, because such narratives are based on a mythology of defensive distortions.

• • •

Narratives and psychological defenses work together to create a psychological lens that can distort our perceptions of reality to the point that fictions become facts and we defend the indefensible. Privilege is the final defense of social powerarchies and it is the topic of the next chapter. Privilege both adds to these psychological distortions and provides a structure with which they become systematized and actionable and through which they become integrated into not only our consciousness but also our policies and practices.

CHAPTER 6

The Power of Privilege

When you're accustomed to privilege, equality feels like oppression.

–ANONYMOUS

"Why?" asks Kimberle Crenshaw to the sea of faces undulating around the little red dot that marks the center of the island she stands on, delivering her TEDWomen speech.[1] "Why does a frame matter?" She's discussing the 1976 class-action discrimination suit led by a black woman named Emma DeGraffenreid against General Motors, for segregating its workforce by both race and gender. "After all, an issue that affects black people and an issue that affects women, wouldn't that necessarily include black people who are women and women who are black people?" Attorney-activist Crenshaw (who was mentioned in chapter 1) explains that how you answer this question depends on your frame. Emma's suit was dismissed because, although GM in fact did not hire black women, it *did* hire black people and it *did* hire women. (It hired white and black men for maintenance and industrial jobs, and white women for reception and secretarial jobs.) But the policymakers at GM (and the courts) didn't have a frame for—or understanding of—how being both black *and* a woman created a distinct social category that created a distinct form of oppression that if not identified, could not be adequately addressed. Crenshaw coined the term *intersectionality* to describe this intersection of oppressions, providing a new frame that has helped lay the groundwork for understanding and challenging privilege.[2]

But what, exactly, is privilege?[3] In powerarchies, privileges are advantages that are granted to the group or individual with more power, while they are denied to others. Privilege, the third defense of powerarchies, keeps some people invested in maintaining power over others and makes it easy for them to do so, as privilege increases the likelihood that they will be successful in life and will have more power—more ability to influence and control others. At the same time, withholding privileges from, or disadvantaging, those with less power decreases the likelihood that these individuals will be successful or able to influence or control others. The more privileges we have, the more successful (and powerful) we become and the more often we get the message that we're worthy, so our belief in our ability to accomplish what we set out to do increases. And the more disadvantaged we are, the less likely we are to succeed or to believe in ourselves.

Privileges thus help ensure that powerarchies are self-perpetuating. For example, someone who was born into economic privilege is more likely to be healthy (having access to wholesome nutrition and medicine) and well educated, to have powerful networks that provide them with career opportunities with which they can attain higher positions of power and influence, and to be encouraged to believe in themselves (which research shows is a key determining factor in one's ability to be successful[4]), while the opposite is true for someone who was born into economic disadvantage.

An excellent metaphor for understanding privilege likens it to an intergenerational relay race. Those born into positions of privilege (economic, racial, gender, and so forth) start out close to, or even at, the finish line and don't need to rely on merit to reach their goals, whereas those who are born into disadvantaged positions start behind everyone else, having to work harder to try to get ahead and often ending up unable to lessen the gap.[5]

PRACTICAL AND PSYCHOLOGICAL PRIVILEGE

Privilege is maintained on both a practical, or structural, level and on a psychological level. Practical and psychological privilege are woven together to create an ignorance of, investment in, and even dependence on unjust power imbalances.

Practical privilege is the actualizing of the myths of social powerarchies by establishing them as policies and protocols and institutionalizing the very practices that sustain unjust power imbalances. For example, certain policies and legislation prevent people who are not cisgender from marrying or benefiting from tax reductions or being able to immigrate to another country when they're in an international relationship. **Psychological privilege** results from turning the myths that obscure and justify privilege into narratives that teach us to buy into the very assumptions and attitudes that help the structures of privilege remain unchallenged. For example, the narrative that transgender and gender-nonconforming people are "deviant" and thus not deserving of the same rights as cisgender people has prevented cisgender and noncisgender people alike from challenging unjust legislation and policies.

The practical privileges granted to members of dominant groups are countless, and they begin even before birth. For example, nutrition and stress affect fetal development, and these factors are directly related to how much access a mother has to proper health care and support, which are in direct proportion to her socioeconomic status, particularly in countries like the United States where such services are largely privatized.[6]

Many, perhaps most, privileges, however, are psychological, and these advantages—or the lack thereof—shape our lives and societies in powerful ways. As we discussed in chapter 5, social powerarchy narratives teach us, for instance, to think of ourselves as attractive or unattractive, as strong or weak, as having valid or invalid needs, and as worthy or unworthy—"better" or "worse" than others. In one study, researchers gave black five-year-old girls two dolls, one white and one black, and asked them to say which one they preferred. Most girls chose the white one, saying that the white doll was "nice" while the black one was "bad."[7]

When we have the privilege of seeing our experience more accurately reflected and validated in mainstream culture, we learn to see ourselves as more nuanced and capable. In popular culture, for instance, representations of white people's experiences dominate the media and reflect complex (rather than simplistic or stereotypical) white characters and white struggles. White people (especially economically advantaged, cisgender, heterosexual men) learn, for instance, that even if they do bad things, that doesn't necessarily make them a bad person. They learn that the things that cause them distress—such as having to manage the demanding workload that comes with attending a private university or with corporate leadership—are indeed distressing and that their reactions to these events make sense. In short, when the mainstream culture reflects and validates our experience, we get the message that our experience matters. We learn that our dreams are valid and that if we try to achieve them, we can. We learn that our thoughts, feelings, and desires are more valid and more normal than those of others. We learn that we're more worthy.

Of course, we are more than just the roles we play in social powerarchies; we may be privileged but still feel powerless in many ways. This is because in a world governed by social powerarchies, our deeper, authentic needs are rarely met. Social powerarchies, which are inherently nonrelational, prevent us from relating to ourselves and others in the ways we need to in order to cultivate the kind of genuine connection and closeness that would bring a sense of satisfaction and true empowerment. Our privilege makes us feel compelled to maintain our privileged status, and although it enables us to get some of our needs met, fulfilling such needs always comes at the expense of others. And as long as we have bought into the tenets of a system that defines "enough" superficially—as based on what we have rather than who we are—we can never feel quite secure in ourselves. Social powerarchies ultimately harm all of us by conditioning us to relate to others and ourselves in inauthentic, dysfunctional, and destructive ways.

THE THREE KEY FEATURES OF PRIVILEGE

Privilege is like a cognitive impairment that hampers our ability to think objectively and to act compassionately. It is distinguished by three key features: people with privilege take up space, it is invisible to those who have it, and it is rarely examined or relinquished without resistance.

People with Privilege Take Up Space

One implicit rule of powerarchies that is expressed through privilege is that people with privilege are allowed to take up the space of others; they feel entitled to cross another's or others' boundaries. Boundaries are the lines delineating our physical, mental, or emotional space—our personal space. All living beings have boundaries, and when those boundaries are not respected, suffering and harm can result.

There is a wide range of ways in which we can cross boundaries. We cross physical boundaries when we tell our partner what they can or can't wear, or when we stand too close to someone or subject others to our loud music, or when we invade and occupy others' land, or when we dump toxic wastes into rivers and streams, or when we take the fur and flesh of other species to use for our own. We cross psychological boundaries when we tell another or others that their perceptions are wrong—when we invalidate their thoughts, opinions, or observations—or when we dominate a conversation and take up all the verbal space. We cross sexual boundaries when we make "cat calls" (when we engage in sexual street harassment) or when we try to coerce those with less power to engage with us sexually. We cross emotional boundaries when we tell another person that they're overreacting when their emotional response isn't what we think it should be.

When we have privilege, we are usually unaware of the fact that we are crossing another's boundaries, and if we do become aware of it, we typically feel that it's okay for us to do so. We may even feel offended by those who point out our boundary violation. For example, few men likely realize the discomfort or distress that their "cat calls" elicit, and when the woman on the receiving end responds by asking them to stop, or even by ignoring them, they may take offense and respond by directing a sexist slur, such as "bitch," at her, thus reasserting—rather than reflecting on—their male privilege. Or when someone visits a friend who has a new kitten, even if the kitten is huddled in the corner of the room, fearful of being handled, they may nevertheless grab her, completely unaware that they are violating the kitten's boundary.

When our own space is invaded, however, we tend to notice it immediately. For example, when someone stands too close to us or touches us when we haven't invited physical contact or revs their motorcycle outside our bedroom window when we're trying to sleep, we often have an instantaneous awareness of such a boundary violation, though the person crossing the boundary is probably oblivious to it.[8]

Privilege Is Invisible to Those Who Have it

Because most of us are unaware of our privilege, despite the fact that we all have certain privileges—and thus a certain amount of power—we don't actually *feel* powerful.[9] In fact, many of us feel that we don't have enough power, especially if we are struggling financially or otherwise in our lives. When others try to point out our privilege to us, highlighting, for example, our white privilege or male privilege and asking us to relinquish some of it, we can feel misunderstood and react defensively: if we don't feel powerful, how can we be expected to "give up" power in a system that seems unfairly balanced against *us*?

One way to appreciate how it's possible to have privilege and still feel disadvantaged is to imagine, as blogger Sian Ferguson suggests, that we're on a long bicycle trek with a friend, and we have different types of bikes and take different routes. Our friend's bike is a three-speed, whereas ours is a ten-speed. Our friend's route is all uphill, whereas ours is only sometimes uphill. The fact that our friend has a harder time than we do doesn't change the fact that it's hard for us, but it also doesn't mean that we suffer equally or that we face the same obstacles.[10]

We rarely become aware of our privilege until something forces us to truly grasp the experience of others who have less privilege than we do. Many of us from economically advantaged countries, for example, don't see the advantages we have until we travel to a country where we witness the abject poverty of much of the rest of the world. (Of course, we may have a similar experience if we witness poverty in our own country.) Before we traveled, we may have actually felt as though our lifestyle was substandard, having compared ourselves to those with a standard of living above ours, such as the celebrities and television characters whose lifestyles are held up for all to see and strive for. And the larger the number of dominant groups we belong to, the more our privilege feels normal and natural, simply the way things are and the way things are meant to be—just as the more we live among others in an economically advantaged country (or social circle), the more normalized our wealthy lifestyle becomes and the more invisible the bubble we are in. So a paradox of privilege is that the more of it we have, the less we see it.

Once we've become aware of our privilege, we can begin to examine it. Examining our privilege means developing a deeper understanding of its nature, expression, and particular manifestations in ourselves. This enables us to change our relationship with our privilege so that we don't use it to reinforce oppression (and ideally we use it in the service of social transformation).

Privilege Is Rarely Relinquished Willingly

One reason why privilege is difficult to challenge is that the narratives that maintain privilege teach us to believe that all (or nearly all) privileges are earned—and therefore just. So when privilege *is* questioned, this act is seen as *un*just and is met with anger. Such anger is defensive in nature: it emerges in order to defend privilege. So those with privilege feel entitled not only to their privilege but also to not having their privilege questioned; one hallmark of privilege is feeling entitled not to see or examine it.[11] Indeed, otherwise open- and fair-minded individuals can become defensive to the point of utter irrationality when a particular privilege they hold comes into question. Such defensiveness makes it especially hard to raise awareness of and discuss privilege and therefore to work toward transforming powerarchies.

Defensive reactions are marked by a lack of curiosity and, perhaps most notably, a lack of empathy. When we're defensive, we're in a state of heightened arousal, meaning that our fight-or-flight response is activated and we have less access to our prefrontal cortex, which, as noted, is the part of our brain that's responsible for rational thinking.[12] This automatic response helps keep us alive; it's an instinctive reaction to danger that enables us to immediately deal with a threat. However, it doesn't serve us when what's needed is rational self-reflection. When we're in a state of defensiveness, we are also less spacious. We tend to fill space (and invade that of others) with our own opinions, feelings, and sense of righteousness rather than create space for learning and understanding. We are less likely to give others the benefit of the doubt and more apt to cling to narratives that serve to maintain a power-over dynamic that privileges us at the expense of others. This is one reason why people who have little to no literacy regarding systemic oppression and the privileges they have been afforded feel entitled to tell others who have such awareness that they don't know what they're talking about[13]—and to not see the utter hubris of their position.

Our defensiveness often continues unchecked, in large part because we fail to see it for what it is. Our privilege distorts our perceptions such that we genuinely believe we're knowledgeable and open when in fact we're uninformed and unreceptive: it causes us both to feel more literate than we actually are about the oppression our privilege defends and (as with dominant narratives) to mistake fact for opinion and opinion for fact. For example, a nondisabled manager who's asked to make changes to meet the needs of an employee suffering from depression and who has no professional experience dealing with mental illness may nevertheless insist that such changes are unnecessary. The manager may believe themselves to be far more informed about the nature of depression and the needs of those suffering from it than they actually are. And even when the depressed individual and the mental health professional who'd advocated for the changes provide clinical information about depression, the manager may treat these facts as opinions and their own opinion as facts, rendering productive dialogue impossible. This conflation of the subjective and objective is often the reason why some privileged individuals use their own, personal experience to invalidate that of millions of others, as when a man who was raised in a family of "strong women" or who has struggled to get dates insists that women have more social power than men. Our privilege can make us feel entitled to dismiss or ignore an entire issue, or even a social justice movement, based simply on our own anecdotal experience.

In many ways, privilege is the glue that holds powerarchies together. And privilege is what causes some of the very people who might otherwise work to transform such systems to end up supporting them. Privilege is one of the central factors that prevents logical discussion and maintains widespread injustice. Without our realizing it, our privilege causes us to defend, rather than challenge, oppression.

THE MYTH OF MERITOCRACY

The assumption that the privileges granted to powerholders are due to merit rather than to luck—that they are earned rather than inherited from an unjust system—is central to keeping social powerarchies intact. This *myth of meritocracy*—the belief that ability and hard work are always fairly rewarded—causes members of dominant groups to feel deserving of their success and causes members of nondominant groups to feel that their lack of success is their own fault, and it keeps everyone from seeing that the system is set up to maintain privileges and power imbalances that benefit some at the expense of others. Consider, for example, how members of disadvantaged socioeconomic groups who struggle to feed their families tend to believe that their own shortcomings are the reason for their hardship[14] (when they haven't been encouraged to blame a convenient scapegoat, such as immigrants). If they were to recognize the real reason—the fact that they are on the losing end of a system that's unfairly rigged—they would probably feel angry at the injustice of their circumstances rather than blame themselves and feel ashamed.

The myth of meritocracy is also the foundation on which neoliberal ideologies and policies—those that favor free-market capitalism—stand, and when this myth is exposed and recognized, it becomes clear that neoliberalism is unlikely to lead to a more just and equitable social order. Indeed, while the main objective of progressive social policies is to help offset the inherent power imbalance in social powerarchies—to offer subsidies and supports that help lessen the gap between members of privileged and disadvantaged social groups—neoliberal policies typically seek to remove such provisions.

A fundamental difference between left- and right-wing thought is that the left tends to recognize the role of systems in general, and of powerarchies in particular, in shaping social dynamics. Naturally, those with such awareness are more likely to support a political orientation that reflects this understanding.

Often, however, critics on the right reverse such cause and effect. For example, it is not uncommon for them to argue that social science departments—a source of legitimation for progressive policies—are influenced by a left-wing bias. This argument is based on the facts that most faculty in the social sciences identify as left-leaning,[15] and most social scientists accept powerarchies as legitimate social phenomena. The argument reflects the assumption that social scientists' progressive orientation causes them to believe in the existence of institutionalized power imbalances that unjustly privilege some at the expense of others—that the reason social scientists accept systems of oppression as valid is because they are left-leaning in the first place. However, it is far more likely that the opposite is true: social scientists' understanding of systems of oppression is what leads them to support progressive politics. Consider, for example, how Galileo, who, following in the footsteps of his predecessor Copernicus, argued against geocentricism (the belief that the other planets and sun revolve around the earth) and for the progressive theory of heliocentrism (the belief that the earth and other planets revolve around the sun). It was not Galileo's progressive orientation that caused him to support heliocentrism, but rather his scientific understanding that led to his progressive orientation.

DECREASING THE POWER OF PRIVILEGE THROUGH INCREASING AWARENESS

If we wish to help transform the dynamics of privilege and oppression, we must change our relationship with our privilege. And one essential way to do this is to become *privilege literate*.[16]

Whereas linguistic literacy is the ability to recognize letters as well as the ability to understand the meaning of the words they create, **privilege literacy** is knowing the facts about privilege (about the oppression the privilege defends and about the structure of the privilege itself), as well as understanding the meaning of those facts. Privilege literacy is awareness, which is both an intellectual and an emotional state. When we are privilege literate, we are informed about the nature and structure of our privilege, and we empathize with those who are impacted by it.

Being privilege literate enables us to recognize the specific manifestations of different oppressions that are often too subtle to detect without our having been informed about them, such as the tendency of men to leave emotional labor[17] and other "caregiving" tasks, such as providing food and drinks and cleaning up after events, to the women in a mixed-gender office; or that of Westerners to avoid eye contact with, and thus render invisible, Muslim women wearing a hijab. When we have an understanding of the nature of privilege, we are more likely to accept that we have unseen biases and are less likely to try to defend them.

Moreover, if those of us promoting countersystems don't understand powerarchies beyond the specific one we are targeting, we risk re-creating problematic power-over dynamics in our outreach, and those who are natural allies to our cause will be unlikely to support it. For example, if white feminists promote an agenda that doesn't account for the experiences of women of color, the white feminists not only end up reinforcing racism but also turn off many people who are naturally allied with feminist values. And just as vegan advocates can develop gender, race, and class analyses so that they don't use sexist, racist, or classist messaging or approaches in their outreach, so, too, can feminists examine their own carnism so that they reduce, and ideally eliminate, their support of nonhuman animal exploitation as they work to end the exploitation inherent in patriarchy. Although we obviously have limited time and energy and cannot be active in all causes at once, we can commit to ensuring that our own work supports that of other groups or, at the very least, doesn't come at a cost to those others.

Making a commitment to an ongoing development of privilege literacy is a critical step to take for any of us in a powerholding position, if we wish to help transform systems of oppression. And as rational and straightforward as this suggestion sounds, heeding it is the exception rather than the rule, because the nature of privilege is such that it causes those of us who have it to deny and defend it.

• • •

Understanding powerarchies and the mechanisms they use to maintain themselves helps us not only to dismantle such systems but also to create systems that are not oppressive in nature. In the next chapter, we will explore these alternatives to powerarchies, and discuss the challenges and opportunities that may accompany working toward new systems of power.

CHAPTER 7

Transforming Power

Every thought you produce, anything you say, any action you do,
it bears your signature.

–THICH NHAT HANH

There is a Buddhist adage that says we all have within us the seeds of greed, hatred, and desire, as well as the seeds of love, compassion, and empathy. Our job is just to water the right seeds. In other words, what we attend to will grow.

Ending oppression requires the dismantling of powerarchies and the transformation of power dynamics on all three levels: social, interpersonal, and intrapersonal. To this end, it is important to understand the structure and nature not only of powerarchies and power-over dynamics but also of the alternatives to powerarchies—power-with systems and power-with dynamics. With such understanding, we can be more intentional in which seeds we choose to water.

POWER-WITH SYSTEMS AND
PSEUDO POWER-WITH SYSTEMS

Power-with systems[1] are organized around the power-with model, which has at its core the practice of integrity; thus I sometimes refer to them as systems of integrity. Unlike powerarchies, which are structured to maintain unjust power imbalances and are dependent on myths and defenses, systems of integrity are structured to balance power and are based on the core moral values of compassion and justice.[2] Whereas powerarchies are nonrelational, closed systems that invalidate anything that challenges their status quo, systems of integrity are relational, open systems that welcome examination from within and outside themselves and are structured to grow and evolve. And, of course, unlike powerarchies, which are disempowering and disconnecting and are based on the belief in a hierarchy of moral worth, systems of integrity are empowering and connecting, and honor the dignity of all beings. In short, systems of integrity are organized around the types of behaviors and qualities that are the opposite of those of powerarchies.

Sometimes systems of integrity are countersystems, such as feminism[3] or veganism, that emerged in reaction to social powerarchies. Other times, a system of integrity may have developed independently of an overt social powerarchy, as with Buddhist monk Thich Nhat Hanh's Order of Interbeing, a system that emphasizes collectivism, compassion, and curiosity.[4] Regardless of how they emerge, systems of integrity differ from powerarchies in both content (their focus or objective) and process (how their proponents relate and communicate).

In short, systems of integrity are organized around balancing power, honoring dignity, and practicing integrity toward individuals and for the greater good. For example, the US civil rights movement was founded on the beliefs that power should be assigned more equitably among members of different ethnic groups, that people of all ethnicities have the same intrinsic worth and therefore deserve equal moral consideration, and that racist attitudes and practices are antithetical to the integrity of individuals and of society as a whole.[5]

Certain powerarchies look like systems of integrity because they have the content of what one would expect from a system of integrity, even though the process of these systems is based on power-over dynamics. So although the systems may have the stated goals of balancing power and increasing integrity, their structure and dynamics are based on the power-over model. Proponents of these

pseudo power-with systems[6] are rarely aware that the content and process of such systems are not aligned. However, recognizing these systems for what they are is important if we hope to avoid perpetuating powerarchy.

The following table shows the key features that differentiate a powerarchy from a system of integrity.

Powerarchy	System of Integrity
Power over	Power with
Disempowerment	Empowerment
Disconnection	Connection
Insecurity	Security
Shame/grandiosity	Pride/humility
Competition (win-lose)	Cooperation (win-win)
Violates integrity	Reflects integrity
Unjust power imbalances	Just distribution of power
Harms dignity	Honors dignity
Relational dysfunction	Relational health
Violates boundaries	Honors boundaries
Fosters insecure attachment	Fosters secure attachment
Trauma	Love
Hierarchy of moral worth	All equally morally worthy
Closed system	Open system
Nonrelational	Relational
Based on myths	Based on awareness

Fundamentalist Systems

Fundamentalism is the strict adherence to a set of basic principles—a set of beliefs with associated values—that have been interpreted literally and narrowly. It is characterized by the rejection of a diversity of opinions or interpretations.[7] Beliefs are typically seen not as beliefs but as ultimate truths. Fundamentalism is therefore not about the content of a system but rather about its process. It is not about specific beliefs but about the process of relating to those beliefs.

In a fundamentalist system, one either agrees with the accepted beliefs and is "right" or does not agree and is "wrong." Fundamentalists don't think "We have different beliefs" but rather "Your beliefs are wrong." Whereas facts can be objectively right or wrong—accurate or inaccurate—beliefs are, by definition, subjective. They are conclusions drawn based on an understanding and interpretation of facts. Clearly, certain beliefs are more grounded in and supported by factual accuracy than are others, but when we talk about beliefs as right and wrong, we are inevitably talking about moral judgments, not about statements of fact.

Fundamentalism therefore creates a perception of "us versus them" and places "them" on a lower rung of a perceived moral hierarchy. Indeed, fundamentalists are ideological purists, and when ideological purity is a core value, then anything that deviates from it tends to be perceived as defiled, degraded—as morally inferior. Fundamentalist systems are powerarchies: they are based on many of the same principles and practices that inform powerarchy.

Fundamentalist systems are sometimes formed by groups within social justice movements that split off from the broader movements, often because of ideological or strategic disagreements. (Often such groups are more radical than the mainstream movement, but radicalization does not automatically translate to fundamentalism.) It is understandable how these fundamentalist systems can form: proponents of countersystems are often those who have been oppressed by a social powerarchy, whose beliefs and values have been chronically invalidated, and who have felt consistently shamed and silenced. Thus they may well need to create a strong in-group identity to assert their position and to adhere more intensely to their values and beliefs. However, regardless of why a fundamentalist system develops, whenever powerarchy is used to challenge powerarchy, we end up with more of the same.

Traumatic Systems

Sometimes, a power-with countersystem can evolve into a "traumatic system," particularly when the social powerarchy being challenged causes extensive violence. Proponents of the countersystem can develop posttraumatic stress from experiencing or witnessing the violence,[8] and the traumatic dynamics they end up engaging in can easily turn the power-with system into a powerarchy. Indeed, trauma is contagious: traumatized people often relate to others in such a way as to trigger them to also develop symptoms of trauma.[9]

Symptoms of posttraumatic stress include chronic workaholism, dysregulated emotions (feeling "too much" or "not enough," or swinging between extremes), intrusive thoughts, misanthropy, survivor guilt (the guilt one feels when one has survived a traumatic event while others perished), a sense of shame and/or grandiosity, and burnout. Perhaps most notably, posttraumatic stress can lead to the development of a trauma narrative, which, as we discussed in chapter 5, causes us to perceive and relate to the world as though it were divided into victims, perpetrators, and heroes, and to treat others and ourselves accordingly.

Many proponents of countersystems who have been traumatized struggle with feeling that they are not good enough and not doing enough to stop the suffering; and in an attempt to offset their guilt and shame, they neglect their own needs. However, attending to one's needs is essential for becoming **resilient**, being able to withstand and bounce back from stress (traumatic or otherwise)—and, ultimately, for maintaining a sense of connection.[10] Thus those whose trauma has remained unaddressed can relate to others in a way that weakens the others' resilience (shaming them or encouraging them to overwork, for example), creating a vicious cycle of power-over dynamics that eventually leads to the creation of a powerarchy.[11]

There is much overlap between traumatic and fundamentalist systems. One could even say that traumatic systems are a type of fundamentalist system (though not all fundamentalist systems may necessarily be traumatic).

Pseudo Power-With Systems and Distorted Perceptions of Power

Sometimes a powerarchy presents itself as a power-with system because its purported goal is balancing power, even though the underlying goal of the system is to maintain or increase an existing power imbalance. Proponents of such pseudo power-with systems no doubt rarely, if ever, realize that they already have what they're fighting for—or that acquiring more power won't bring them the sense of self-worth they may seek, as it's impossible to feel truly empowered in such a way within a powerarchy.

For example, white supremacists who feel disempowered by the fact that the power differential between white people and people of color has finally begun to lessen (even though the imbalance remains significant) perceive such a shift in race relations as a total overturning of "white power": they actually see white people on the lower end of an unbalanced power dynamic.[12] Similarly, some men seek to establish "all-male clubs" simply because there are "all-female" environments.[13] They assume that measures to create safety (emotional and/or physical) for a group with far less social power and far higher rates of gender-based victimization reflect a total reversal in the gender power differential.

These pseudo power-with systems reflect inaccurate assessments of how power is concentrated and distributed. They are based on distorted perceptions and a lack of data. One way to challenge such systems is to conduct an analysis of current power distributions (to evaluate which group holds more positions of influence in social institutions, whose ideas are more represented throughout such institutions, and who holds economic power) and to assess the historical trend of the power distributions (to determine how long the current dominant group has been the powerholder). The data garnered can be used to encourage proponents of the pseudo power-with system to recognize that their perceptions of power are skewed and to reflect on their existing privilege. Of course, shifting perceptions will take more than presenting data analyses, but gathering accurate information to challenge "false facts" is an important step in the right direction.

POWERARCHY BEGETS POWERARCHY

Gandhi famously said, "As the means, so the ends." In other words, the process we use to accomplish a goal will determine what kind of goal we end up with. Proponents of nonviolent social change have long championed this approach, arguing that we become what we practice. And from a psychological perspective, Gandhi's argument makes sense.

Transforming oppression requires not simply abolishing oppressive policies and practices but transforming oppressive systems—and systems, as we have noted, are psychological in nature. More specifically, systems are relational. Every action we engage in, including thinking, reflects a model of power that informs how we relate to others and ourselves. And every action that is reciprocated becomes an interaction, or a dynamic—a power dynamic. Power dynamics are relational phenomena, and systems (whether they comprise two or two million individuals) are, essentially, aggregates of power dynamics. Therefore, if we wish to transform oppression, we must transform the way we relate.

Moreover, power-over behaviors are contagious. When a power-over behavior is enacted, it almost inevitably triggers a power-over response. In her groundbreaking book, *Dignity*, author Donna Hicks cites myriad studies demonstrating that we are hardwired to respond to affronts to our dignity—which are inherent in power-over behaviors—as though they were assaults on our body.[14] We go into a state of hyperarousal, and our capacity for rational and empathic responding is diminished. Indeed, our automatic tendency, an evolutionary self-protective reaction, is to counterattack, often in like manner. Hicks cites a study by James Gilligan, who asked twenty-five hundred inmates why they felt compelled to kill and was told by the majority of them that it was because they had felt disrespected.[15] And in *Emotional Intelligence*, author Daniel Goleman points out that on a neurobiological level, we are powerfully impacted by relational dynamics: behaviors that cause us to feel demeaned can actually weaken our immune system and, over time, can even reshape our brains.[16] Multiple studies have demonstrated that the way we express ourselves toward others—including through "microexpressions" that are often not even consciously detected by either party—causes others to respond in like kind,[17] and also that, for every "negative" (or power-over) communication, such as being offensive or invalidating, it takes five "positive" (or power-with) ones, such as being affirming or supportive, to offset it.[18] Moreover, a single power-over communication, such as when we are on the receiving end of an insulting email, can diminish our mood and energy level for hours or even days.[19] Some emotional contagion researchers claim that negative (power-over) interactions "spread like the common cold."[20] So power-over dynamics beget power-over dynamics, on a psychological, behavioral, social, and even biological level. Over time, if we practice power over enough in our personal and social systems, it becomes normalized, and our systems become powerarchies. Herein lies the reason why the process is so vital—why the means do indeed powerfully inform the ends—when working toward transforming oppression.

The tendency for power over to re-create itself is also why social problems cannot be solved simply through technological or even rational means. Although technology can certainly play a role in helping create a more just world, without a shift of consciousness from power over to power with, technological innovations can be (and often have been) used to sustain powerarchy. The internet, for example, both empowered Al Qaida and helped mobilize the Arab Spring. And although rationality is critical to transforming oppression, rational solutions to problems of oppression that are conceptualized from within the powerarchical model can easily lead to conclusions that support, rather than challenge, powerarchy.

Indeed, when a powerarchy is used to challenge a powerarchy, the content of the system being challenged may change, but the process does not. It can be helpful think of powerarchy as an entity with a survival instinct (a metaphor akin to that used in chapter 5). To feed itself, powerarchy needs an "other," another individual or group deemed less worthy. It doesn't care who that other is; the other simply exists to keep the power-over dynamic alive, to maintain the power imbalance and the sense of superiority of the powerholding individual or group.[21] So, as long as powerarchy is a system's norm, it will find an outlet somewhere. The victims of the system may change, but the power dynamic remains intact.

As we work toward transforming oppression, situations will inevitably arise when we have to ask ourselves whether, in some cases, our approach must incorporate actions that look like power over. We may, for example, need to enforce power over individuals or groups who are causing harm to others, such as when we prevent hate speech from being carried out. However, even in such circumstances, we can maintain a commitment to power with by trying to ensure that our actions are in the best interest of the integrity of the individuals being impacted as well as of the greater good—that they are designed not simply to reduce harm but also to increase integrity and a balance of power—and that they do not assume a hierarchy of moral worth. For instance, people who promote and implement policies and legislation preventing hate speech can nevertheless honor the dignity of hate speech proponents while keeping their focus on preventing harmful behavior rather than on curtailing "immoral" people. Indeed, experts point out that many people join hate groups in youth, while they're still impressionable, and that, among members of such groups, incidents of childhood physical abuse and psychological maltreatment are higher than average.[22] There are many reasons why individuals are attracted to hate groups, but a key driver is the search for a sense of connection, belonging, power, and personal value. White supremacist leader turned peace activist Christian Picciolini contends that filling these needs and extending compassion to such individuals (while still holding them accountable) are essential to transforming their violent mindset.[23] Further affronts to their dignity would no doubt feed their sense of disconnection, disempowerment, and hate— causing them to feel even more defensive and attached to the powerarchy—and further obstruct justice.

On a practical level, there will be knotty problems to unravel as we work toward such change—needs among individuals and groups will clash, and what is in the best interest of the individual or of the greater good may sometimes be difficult or impossible to determine. But if we approach social change with a commitment to practicing power with, we will be far better able to address these problems in a productive manner that leads to sound solutions.

It's also important to note that not only does powerarchy beget powerarchy but power itself begets powerarchy. Having power tends to corrupt: it distorts our perceptions of ourselves and others such that we often act powerarchically without realizing this fact. So it is important to develop **power literacy**. Power literacy is understanding the nature and structure of power dynamics, including how having, or acquiring, even small amounts of power can affect our thoughts and feelings, driving us to engage in power-over dynamics (it also includes understanding how not having power affects us). Research has shown that when we are in a position of power, we experience diminished empathy; we are less likely to act with integrity; and we are more likely to act in ways that are self-serving, entitled, and impulsive and to justify these behaviors to ourselves and others.[24] If we are not aware of the corrupting influence of power, when we work to challenge powerarchy we are at risk of simply inverting the hierarchical ladder of moral worth.

Each of us has the power to help shift the systems of which we are a part. In order to operate within a system, which is like being in a dance (an analogy we discussed in chapter 3), all members have to be dancing to the same song, doing the same dance steps.[25] For example, we cannot dance with a partner who is waltzing if we're doing the foxtrot. The dance steps, of course, are the roles and rules of the system that we're operating in. To change the dance, we must change our own dance steps—the roles we play and the rules we follow. We obviously have different amounts of power to bring about change in different systems. In a couple system, for example— all power roles being relatively equal—we have much more power to shift the system than we do in a social system. However, when enough individuals in a system change their dance steps, the process of the system is interrupted and the system transforms.

INCREASING RELATIONALITY

Because power-over behaviors are contagious, spreading beyond their immediate systems to re-create themselves elsewhere, it is important that we practice power-with behaviors in our daily interactions, even as we work toward broader social transformation. Promoting compassion and justice in our social outreach while, for example, shaming those who disagree with us on social media sites or belittling our domestic partner is like being an environmentalist who drives a Hummer.

In other words, we must commit to ongoing development of our own relationality, which includes developing **relational literacy**—the ability to understand and express healthy ways of relating, which includes emotional intelligence,[26] self-awareness, mindfulness, and effective communication skills.[27] (We'll discuss most of these factors in this chapter and in chapter 8.) Indeed, most of us have never received a single lesson in how to relate healthfully—despite the fact that we probably had to learn complicated geometry we never needed to use. On top of this, we have been born into a world in which profound relational dysfunction is the norm. So we need to commit to developing our relationality if we wish to shift our own relational dynamics.

This is not to say that those of us who are challenging and/or being harmed by powerarchies should be the ones responsible for transforming them, or that we should strive for moral perfection. It is also not to imply that we all have equal opportunity to practice power-with behaviors; we must have at least some degree of privilege in order to be able to choose how we act, and those with more power to change a system have a greater responsibility to do so. Rather, it is to suggest that, if we wish to help create a world in which people feel less compelled to demean others and are better able to practice integrity, we must help construct a base of dignity on which to build healthy interpersonal and social relationships. And a part of this work is to integrate power-with dynamics in all areas of our life to the best of our ability. Moreover, our personal lives and relationships will be empowered accordingly.

DEVELOPING AWARENESS AND PRACTICING MINDFULNESS

Perhaps the two most important methods for bringing power with into our daily lives are developing awareness and practicing mindfulness, methods that are mutually reinforcing. The more aware (particularly the more self-aware) and mindful we are, the less likely we are to be hijacked by automatic, defensive reactions to power-over dynamics—to catch and spread their contagion—and the more likely we are to practice integrity and to honor others' (and our own) dignity. We are therefore more likely to cultivate empowerment and connection in ourselves, our relationships, and the groups (including the social justice movements) to which we belong. So we can decrease the likelihood that we will wield power over others or that others will wield power over us.

As noted in previous chapters, awareness is essential for diminishing the power of the defenses that maintain powerarchy and therefore for transforming the system. Because powerarchy functions on unexamined myths and implicit rules, becoming aware of the system and the way it influences our interactions is a central part of dismantling it. Raising such awareness is the main objective of this book.

Beyond developing awareness of powerarchy, developing **self-awareness** is a fundamental method for transformation. Studies have shown that high levels of self-awareness are integral to healthy relationships—and to effective leadership,[28] an issue that pertains to all of us who are organizers and ambassadors for social causes. Developing self-awareness, which is the capacity to reflect on our thoughts, feelings, personality, identity, resources, and other aspects of our personal and internal experiences, enables us to be more empowered, connected, and, therefore, relational. When we are more self-aware, we are

- more likely to recognize that we are neither more nor less worthy than others, so we're less likely to feel defensive against, or engage in, power-over behaviors that target self-worth;

- better able to recognize and therefore attend to and communicate our needs, including our relational needs, such as our need for reassurance, connection, or respect, so we are less likely to engage in controlling or manipulative (power-over) behaviors to get our needs met;

- more likely to identify our boundaries, so we're less likely to allow others to violate them;

- less likely to act out defensively (with power over), as we're more open to self-examination and can reflect on, and learn from, our feeling of defensiveness without reacting to it;

- more likely to be accountable when we engage in powerarchical behaviors that harm others and to rectify such behaviors, because we are open to self-examination;

- more in tune with our core moral values, so we are more likely to know when we're not acting in accordance with them;

- more honest with ourselves and open to examining our beliefs, so we're less likely to think dogmatically, and we're more likely to make behavioral choices that reflect what we authentically think and feel, rather than what we've been taught to think and feel;

- and more likely to appreciate how our experience is different from that of others, so we're less likely to assume that others should think, feel, and act as we do and to judge them for being different.

Awareness is perhaps best cultivated through the practice of mindfulness. Mindfulness is both a strategy, or practice, and a state. It is at once a tool for developing awareness and also a state of presence, of being present in the moment.

Multiple studies have demonstrated that practicing mindfulness increases self- and other-awareness and improves relationality.[29] Practicing mindfulness actually rewires the brain so that we become more attentive and focused, less defensive, and more empathic and compassionate.[30] What's more, it enables us to better observe and regulate our emotions to prevent ourselves from getting triggered into hyperarousal. And when we do end up triggered in such a way, we are better able to self-soothe and reduce our hyperarousal so that we regain access to our prefrontal cortex and are more able to think rationally and reconnect with our empathy. Practicing mindfulness also increases resilience, the ability to withstand and bounce back from stress, and it ultimately enables us to be more intentional and less automatic and reactive in our interactions.

Mindfulness can be practiced through any activity, from eating to walking. However, two activities in particular can be especially powerful ways to develop a mindfulness practice: meditation and nonviolent communication. Both of these methods help cultivate our "inner observer," the part of ourselves that objectively and compassionately witnesses our experiences as they unfold. As our inner observer becomes stronger, we create more space between ourselves and our experience—such as our thoughts and feelings, and the behaviors of others—so that we can approach situations more rationally and compassionately.[31] (Setting an alarm to go off several times throughout the day and pausing to nonjudgmentally reflect on your inner experience—asking yourself what you are thinking and feeling—can also help develop your inner observer.)

There are a number of methods for developing a meditation practice. Today, many apps and programs make the process easier than it used to be, and you can tailor your practice to your needs. Even meditating ten minutes a day has been shown to help develop mindfulness.

Nonviolent communication is a method of communication that helps cultivate mindfulness and also reflects and reinforces power-with dynamics. And because we're communicating virtually all the time—with others and also with ourselves, through our internal dialogue—we have ample opportunities to practice this technique. Each time we communicate, no matter how "unmindful" our prior communications have been, we have a new opportunity to practice mindfulness. (Few communications or interactions cause irreversible damage, and at any moment in an interaction we can work toward repair.) We can practice mindfulness when, for example, we're discussing a difference of opinion with our partner, posting a political commentary online, simply paying for our groceries, or sitting quietly reflecting on our day. Indeed, studies have shown that our internal dialogue impacts many aspects of our experience, such as our self-perception and our ability to achieve our goals, and that pausing to notice and, when appropriate, restructure our self-talk so that it's more nonviolent can significantly improve our well-being and relationships.[32] Working to ensure that our internal dialogue is nonviolent may be particularly important when we are occupying disadvantaged positions in a system, whereby we may have internalized oppressive messages about ourselves.

The nonviolent communication method[33] involves identifying our

- observations, which are factual observations of what we notice, without judgment (e.g., "There's no spinach left in the freezer," or "My parents live in Guatemala");
- thoughts, which are our perceptions, opinions, or beliefs (e.g., "I assume you used the last of the spinach and didn't replace it," or "Democracy can never work on a large scale");
- feelings ("I'm feeling frustrated that, for the third time this month, the spinach wasn't replaced and I didn't have it when I needed it," or "I'm hungry");

- and needs ("I'd appreciate it if you made sure to replace the spinach when you use the last of it," or "I need you not to check your phone when I'm talking with you").

Nonviolent communication also involves differentiating these components from one another. So, to communicate nonviolently, we need to objectively reflect on a situation and our experience and to share this information without judgment. In so doing, we automatically communicate more rationally, intentionally, and compassionately. And when we understand the principles and tools of nonviolent communication, we are better able to identify violent communication that may be directed against or about us or our community, thus reducing the chances that we will buy into such messages or end up engaged in dysfunctional conversations.

The good news is that power-with behaviors, like power-over behaviors, are also self-replicating.[34] It can be helpful to pay attention to the company you keep, assessing whether the systems of which you are a part reflect the kinds of behaviors and values you wish to enhance in your life and in the world. Indeed, as your communication becomes more nonviolent, and your state of being becomes more mindful, you may find that your tolerance for toxic or disrespectful communication and ways of being decreases. You may find that you "outgrow" some of your systems as you raise your awareness and increase your level of mindfulness.

• • •

We have discussed the basic nature and structure of powerarchies and of their alternatives, systems of integrity. We've also discussed some of the key reasons it's imperative that we shift our own consciousness and daily behaviors in order to help shift the systems of which we are a part, from powerarchical toward power with, as well as some methods for doing so. Now we will discuss how to help cultivate such a shift based on the specific roles we play in powerarchies, so that we may more effectively prevent and reverse power-over dynamics in our work for social transformation.

CHAPTER 8

Beyond Oppression

All you need to know is that the future is wide open and you are about to create it by what you do.

–PEMA CHÖDRÖN

Although popular culture—at least in many parts of the world—has taught us to believe in the powerarchical myth that we can and should be islands unto ourselves, in truth we are all interconnected within the various systems of which we are a part. We're like spiders running along the strands of a great web of interbeing, every seemingly independent action affecting, and affected by, the whole. Given that we are participants within myriad systems—for better or worse—our choice is not *whether* we participate but *how* we participate. When we understand how to participate in a way that transforms powerarchy, we can be a part of the process of moving beyond oppression.

Moving beyond oppression requires not only a shift of consciousness, from a powerarchical to a power-with mentality (as we discussed in chapter 7), but also a commitment to making specific changes based on our role, or position, and our intention within a given powerarchy. Although collective measures, such as community organizing and political lobbying, are essential, whether and how to carry out such efforts must be determined contextually; such a process goes beyond the scope of this book. So in this chapter, we'll discuss some ways we, as individuals, can help transform powerarchy when we are in a powerholding, or privileged, position;

when we are in either a privileged or oppressed position; and/or when we are acting as advocates, challenging privilege from either of the aforementioned positions.

It's also useful to note that, because powerarchies are traumatic systems, the roles we play in a powerarchy may reflect the roles played in a traumatic event. When we are powerholding, or privileged, we may be in the position of "perpetrator"; when we are oppressed, we may be in the role of "victim"; and when we challenge privilege, we are in the position of "hero"—and we can play the hero role from either of the aforementioned positions such that we offset them (e.g., we can challenge privilege from a position of privilege, acting as an ally; or we can be oppressed and challenge privilege).

TRANSFORMING POWERARCHY
WHEN WE ARE PRIVILEGED

Transforming a powerarchy requires changing how we relate within the system. When we are in a powerholding position, we're in a position of privilege; so to transform powerarchy, we need to transform the way we relate to our privilege. We need to relate to our privilege so that we help offset, rather than reinforce, oppression.

Moreover, as noted in chapter 7, the onus of responsibility for transforming powerarchies must rest with those in positions of greater power. When we are in a position of privilege, we generally have more power to change the system than we would were we in a disadvantaged position. And given that we've been benefiting at the expense of others (whether we've wished this to be the case or not), our working toward rectifying the unfair power imbalance is an important step toward creating a more just system.

Learning and Listening

As we discussed in chapter 6, when we're in a position of privilege it's essential that we commit to developing privilege literacy. And it's important that, as we learn, we not expect those from oppressed groups to become our teachers.[1] Often, we can feel that our mere willingness to learn about our privilege is somehow an act of heroism and that those who are negatively impacted by our privilege should be grateful for the opportunity to try to educate us. Consider, for instance, how the one student in a classroom who's a member of a particular nondominant group (Muslim, genderqueer, etc.) may be expected to represent their entire community by providing their perspective on whatever topic is being discussed, and how such a situation is often seen as an opportunity for them, rather than a burden. But being open to learning about how our privilege has caused us to walk over the rights of others only feels noble because of the entitlement such privilege instills in us; the least we can do is look at what we need to see in order to stop causing harm. To this end, it is our responsibility to get educated. We are simply falling back on our privilege when we put others in the position of having to synthesize and communicate complex interpersonal and social dynamics and structures that they may not have fully thought through themselves and that will inevitably cost them significant time and energy. It's not fair to expect others to give us all the answers or to solve our problems for us. The information is out there for us to find on our own.[2]

Although we must take care not to make others responsible for our education, it's important that we ask questions—questions that help us understand the experiences of others who see our privilege more clearly than we do. Often, when those of us with privilege do ask questions, we do so only to create an opportunity to debate the answers we get and to further justify our privilege. We may, for example, pose hypothetical questions that have little bearing on the issue at hand, such as asking how the social order would be maintained if all people had satisfying jobs and earned a living wage ("Don't we need people to do the work nobody wants to do?"). So we use the conversation not as a forum for examining our privilege but rather as an opportunity to assert and defend it. We may feel that playing devil's advocate is the best way for us to truly under-

stand an issue, but such an approach can easily cause those who
have been chronically invalidated and challenged to feel that they
are being cross-examined and that their reality is being doubted
once again. When communicating with those who are negatively
impacted by our privilege, it's especially important to adapt our conversational style to one that respects their experience, an approach
we'll discuss more fully later in this chapter.

We also need to accept that we do not, and cannot, know what
the experience of others is like unless they tell us—especially when
those others are members of nondominant groups that we don't belong to—and that we very likely know far less than they do when
it comes to their group's experience of power dynamics. Often,
when the subject of our privilege comes up—when, for instance,
we find ourselves in a conversation about gender or race and we're
a member of the dominant group—our tendency is not to listen
and learn but to take on the role of expert, because our privilege
causes us to feel that we know more than we actually do about the
issue at hand. For example, women often find that as soon as they
begin to discuss their experience living in patriarchy, men start ex-
plaining all the ways in which the women are wrong about what
they're perceiving, feeling, or wanting. Sometimes the men also
point out how they, too, have had such an experience, suggesting
that there is no patriarchal power imbalance. For instance, when the
MeToo movement began, in which myriad women spoke out
against high-powered men by whom they'd been sexually harassed
in a culture of rampant sexism and violence against women, some
men who had been victims of sexual harassment claimed it was
likely that many men had also been victimized but were simply not
coming forward—which may be true, but which nevertheless suggested that sexual violence, which is a well-documented gender-
based phenomenon—was somehow gender-neutral.[3] In short, we
should be careful not to define the reality of members of nondominant groups, which is the very tendency our privilege instills in us.

When others point out our privilege, we need to listen to what
they have to say, even if they don't point it out in the most gracious

way. People don't always communicate as effectively as they could, especially when the subject is charged. Nevertheless, we need to listen and to hold off on our tendency to want to make them wrong and poke holes in their argument so as to defend our own (privileged) position. We may not always agree with what we hear, but it's essential that we commit to doing our best to be fully open to the information coming our way. (Of course, our willingness to listen should be within reason. Everyone deserves to be treated with basic respect, and if a conversation is demeaning or otherwise disrespectful—reflecting power-over dynamics—choosing not to engage may well be the choice of integrity.)

We need, in other words, to notice our tendency to feel defensive when we hear about how our privilege impacts others, and not to act on this feeling. We need to know that it's the nature of privilege to cause us to feel attacked whenever we hear about it; to exaggerate the anger of those who are communicating with us; to fail to see their anger as a normal and healthy response to injustice; to deny or minimize their suffering or the injustice caused by our privilege and to grasp at arguments to prove them wrong; and to assume that our dominant narrative is more valid than their nondominant one, when the opposite is more likely to be the case.

Tailoring Our Communication

When discussing our privilege with those who have been harmed by it, our usual ways of communicating are often not sufficient. This is largely because those individuals may have strong emotions, and possibly even posttraumatic reactions, around the issue. Such pain may be the result of the harm and suffering they've endured (or in some cases witnessed). It may also result from having been chronically silenced. Many individuals who have been trying to speak out and have had to face the anger and defensiveness of the dominant, powerarchical culture end up angry and defensive themselves. When people aren't listened to when they talk, especially about matters where the stakes are high, they talk louder and eventually end up yelling. They can also fall into despair, as productive conversation seems hopeless.

The intensity of the pain of members of oppressed groups can also be the result of releasing years (even generations) of emotional repression. It's not uncommon for the painful emotions caused by oppression to be stuffed down, or repressed, at least to some degree, as long as there is no tolerance or space for their expression. People often repress their emotions when they get the message that such emotions are "wrong" (e.g., that what they're emotional about isn't really happening or is their fault) and so they don't feel entitled to feel them. People may also repress their emotions when they believe that it's not safe or useful to feel and express those emotions—when, for example, they will be assaulted for expressing their anger, or nobody will take them seriously and they know that self-expression will cause them to feel even more enraged and despairing. Such a dynamic is perhaps easier to understand in the context of an abusive relationship: as long as the abuser refuses to acknowledge the injustice and harm of their behaviors, the person being abused cannot afford to feel, or to fully feel, their resulting emotions unless they are ready and able to end the relationship. Repressing emotions in order to function is a coping mechanism that enables people to continue in unhealthy systems that they are not free to exit.

Once there is an opening for repressed emotions to emerge, these feelings can come rushing to the surface. This can occur when the denial of those of us who are privileged is pierced, and we are able to acknowledge the pain our actions (or the actions of others who share our privilege) have caused. Often at this point, those who have been harmed by our privilege are still reeling from years of emotional (and sometimes physical) wounding—but we are not sufficiently literate, and we don't realize that the usual ways of communicating are not appropriate and can even be counterproductive. We can see such a phenomenon in the MeToo movement, where a number of men have expressed a genuine desire to engage in productive dialogue, but have found that their attempts to communicate have fueled, rather than offset, the problem.

Because the usual forms of communication often do not work when dialoguing about privilege and oppression, we need some guidelines for such conversations. Understanding the stages of recovery from trauma[4]—stages that may also apply to recovery from oppression—can help guide our communications so that they can be more productive.

Understanding Stages of Recovery from Trauma

Recovery from trauma is a complex process, with stages that are often revisited over time. Here, we'll just briefly define the stages for the purpose of understanding their influence on communication. The first stage of recovery is safety. An individual (or group) who has felt unsafe (emotionally or otherwise) and disempowered—hallmarks of both traumatic and oppressive experiences—needs to know, first and foremost, that they won't be further harmed. In the second stage, the victim(s) acknowledge and express the emotions related to the trauma (which is only possible if safety has been established). In the third and final stage, the victim(s) reconnect with others—and it is only at this point that the usual ways of communicating with the victim(s) are appropriate.

When an individual (or group) first begins raising awareness of our privilege, it is often during stage 1 or 2 of recovery, and it is therefore not the time to employ our usual means of communicating, as not enough healing has taken place. This simply means that we should talk less and listen more. And when we do talk, it should be primarily in the interest of learning more about the other's experience (e.g., "What has it been like for you to experience this?"). Playing devil's advocate or debating—even if we are truly on a quest for truth—may well cause the other to feel that their reality is being defined or to otherwise feel invalidated, as such behaviors mirror the very methods that have been used to maintain the oppression they're speaking out about. Looking again to the MeToo example, we can perhaps better understand why many well-intentioned men who attempted to join the conversation felt frustrated at what they believed was an expectation that they stifle their curiosity and suppress their questions. They therefore ended up assuming that forums for discussion were preventing a diversity of opinions, and tensions escalated.

The early stages of recovery are also not the time to talk too much about ourselves, including about our own concerns regarding the problems our privilege has caused. Doing so can be perceived as (and can in fact be) placing ourselves back in the privileged position of being the focus of attention, of being "centered." Centering ourselves can also be seen as a demand for empathy, and for many people who have been oppressed, empathy for those who have contributed to the oppression (even if such contribution was not direct or intentional) can be dangerous, as members of oppressed groups are socialized to overempathize with members of privileged groups and to deny their own perspective and needs (an issue discussed later in this chapter).

In the early stages of recovery, our focus should be primarily on listening—listening deeply, with the goal of fully understanding the experiences of those who have been oppressed. Of course, listening in such a way is important in all stages of recovery, but by the third stage, listening can be accompanied more fully by other forms of communicating.

TRANSFORMING POWERARCHY WHEN WE ARE PRIVILEGED OR OPPRESSED

All of us straddle multiple realities, playing various roles within a given system. We all have some forms of privilege, and we all belong to some oppressed groups. (Because powerarchies comprise systems involving nonhumans, even people who belong to multiple oppressed groups nevertheless retain human privilege.) And, as discussed previously, we can challenge privilege from either of the aforementioned positions. Although certain methods for transforming powerarchy discussed in this chapter are more appropriate and impactful when we employ them from a particular position we're occupying (when, for example, we're powerholders, in a position of privilege), most methods are still at least somewhat applicable regardless of our position. However, one method in particular is perhaps equally appropriate to employ, whether we're privileged, oppressed, or challenging privilege: compassionate witnessing.

Compassionate witnessing, a term coined by psychologist Kaethe Weingarten, entails paying attention and listening with empathy and compassion and without judgment.[5] When we compassionately witness another, our goal is not to be right, to win an argument, or even to fix a problem. It is simply to understand the truth of the other's experience. When we compassionately witness another, we are saying, "I see you: I empathize and I care," as occurred during the process of truth and reconciliation in South Africa and in the BBC program *Facing the Truth*, in which sessions between victims and perpetrators of Northern Ireland's political conflict were mediated.[6] Of course, compassionate witnessing in itself does not guarantee an ideal outcome of a situation, but it is a necessary step in the process of reconciliation or healing.

To be truly seen is a great gift, one that is sorely lacking in most of our lives and in the culture at large. It is especially lacking among those who have less power in powerarchies, as their experiences are underrepresented and misrepresented and thus rendered less visible or invisible.

Compassionate witnessing is a central practice of power with. We feel validated when we feel accepted for who we are, when we don't feel judged for what we think and feel. And when we feel validated, we feel unashamed and worthy—we feel that we matter. Compassionate witnessing is therefore the antidote to shame. When we're told that our feelings or experience are "wrong," we get the message that we don't matter. When we're not responded to when we reach out to another, we get the message that we don't matter. By contrast, when we're met with compassion and empathy, we are empowered.

Compassionate witnessing can transform our lives and our world. When we compassionately witness ourselves, we deepen our connection with ourselves, and we increase our integrity and decrease our shame. When we practice compassionate witnessing toward others, we empathize with those who are suffering and help create a more just and compassionate world. Indeed, virtually every atrocity is made possible by a populace that turns away from a reality they feel is too painful to face. And virtually every social transformation is made possible because a group of people chooses to bear witness and encourages others to bear witness as well. Social transformation requires that we shift from a culture of oppression to a culture of compassionate witnessing.

Compassionate witnessing can also help us develop healthy psychological boundaries, which are essential for healthy interpersonal dynamics and relationships. Psychological boundaries enable us to be at once connected and protected.[7] When relating within a powerarchy, those with privilege tend to have boundaries that are too rigid: their boundaries don't allow in information that challenges their narratives or that enables them to identify and empathize with others whose experiences they have not been sensitized to. Members of oppressed groups tend to have boundaries that are too porous: their boundaries cause them to distrust their own narrative when it competes with the dominant one and to overidentify and empathize with others, especially powerholders. Those with less power therefore often need to increase their self-witnessing so that they don't overfocus on others and allow the others' version of reality to define their own.[8]

TRANSFORMING POWERARCHY WHEN WE ARE ACTING AS ADVOCATES

We're in a position of advocacy when we're challenging privilege, whether we're doing so as members of the group the privilege has harmed or as members of the privileged group itself. Regardless of our power role, when we're advocating to transform powerarchy, there are some strategies we can employ to increase the chances that our efforts will be successful.

Being Careful with Calling Out

Sometimes, those of us who are members of oppressed groups (and advocates for these groups) can, in an attempt to shore up our boundaries, develop a reactionary psychological rigidity. As we strive to balance power, we may cling too rigidly to our own reactionary narrative about people who belong to dominant groups—about those people's motivations, character, internal experience, and so on. In so doing, we end up defining the reality of members of dominant groups, practicing power over them and invalidating and shaming them.[9] Call-out culture[10] is an example of this phenomenon, whereby the intention to raise awareness of oppression by pointing out instances of oppressive behavior, often using social media, is frequently carried out in such a way as to punish or chastise rather than to educate.

For example, a number of concepts and terms have emerged to highlight and challenge the defensiveness caused by privilege. However, although these expressions are important means of initiating productive conversations, when the process by which they are implemented reflects power over rather than power with, they end up instead creating destructive dialogue, often causing those who are being asked to change their relationship with their privilege to feel that they're in a no-win situation. For instance, if a powerholder doesn't speak out in an online discussion about oppression, they may be told they're hiding behind their privilege and not an ally. If they do speak out—even if they make it clear they're speaking from the only position they can, their own experience—they may be told they're centering themselves or, worse, erasing the voices of those with less power, and that they shouldn't be speaking. If, when they speak out, they make a comment that reflects an ignorance of their privilege, as all of us inevitably do, their character may be attacked (they may be called racist, sexist, ableist, etc.). If they feel ashamed or hurt, they may be told they are "crying male tears" (that their shame is exaggerated or fabricated). If they explain their reasoning for an opinion or statement, they may be told they're being defensive. If they've been on the receiving end of disrespectful, inflammatory comments and they ask to be spoken to respectfully, they may be told they're tone policing. (Note that tone policing is stating that a person should not communicate when they're feeling or expressing emotion; this is not the same as requesting that communication be respectful, which is healthful and necessary for productive conversation.) Thus we must remember to allow others to be the experts on their own experience, lest we communicate (and send a message to onlookers) that defining someone's reality and making otherwise disrespectful comments are acceptable behaviors—and lest we use the tools that were constructed to support power with as weapons to defend power over.

Of course, call-out culture emerged in large part to counteract the culture of privilege that makes people feel entitled to say whatever they want and not get called on it. However, how we talk about privilege matters. No matter how "right" we may feel our countersystem is, facts are rarely sufficient to sell an ideology. Debating facts or simply stating the rightness of our position is unlikely to win us supporters. If we fail to appreciate the psychology of those with whom we communicate, we will likely increase their defensiveness rather than their awareness. For example, despite having identified the fragility, or heightened sensitivity, of members of dominant groups when it comes to examining their privilege, many social justice advocates blatantly ignore this fact, calling out and shaming those who are most likely to react defensively to such shame (and most people *are* fragile when it comes to being shamed). Rather than use information about fragility to reach out more effectively, some social justice advocates do the very things that tend to trigger shame and defensiveness. It's like holding a glass vase that's full of cracks and, instead of handling it extra gently, slamming it down and then getting angry when it breaks. If we hope to challenge privilege, we must be especially careful to frame our message in a way that takes into account people's sensitivity around the issue.

Some readers may argue that attending to the fragility of members of dominant groups shifts yet another burden from those who are privileged onto others, making others responsible for "coddling" people who already have an unfair advantage. It can also be argued that many powerholders use their fragility as a way to avoid being held accountable for their actions; their strong emotional reaction to having their privilege pointed out often makes others too uncomfortable to bring up the topic. These arguments are true. It is also true that if we wish to be effective in challenging privilege, we must relate to people as they are, not as we wish they were. If we ignore psychological realities because we don't like such realities, we can sabotage our efforts for change. Furthermore, it is entirely possible to be gentle *and* firm when we challenge privilege. We can be cautious not to trigger shame while still holding people accountable and being clear about our demands, which is the respectful approach no matter who we're relating to. Is it fair that members of nondominant groups must work to bridge the ideological and communication gaps to try to balance power? Of course not. But unlike powerholders, members of nondominant groups have lived in two worlds—they have been immersed in the world of the dominant culture and have had to learn its language in order to survive in it—and, on top of this, they are motivated to bring about change to a degree that most members of dominant groups simply are not.

Avoiding Shaming

Many advocates use shaming as a tactic because they believe, incorrectly, that shame will motivate people to change—and on top of this, they underestimate the consequences of shaming powerholders. Studies have shown that shaming behaviors—which are those that harm dignity—trigger a defensive response that reduces the likelihood that a person will be open to making positive changes.[11] And although some people claim that they were inspired to change by having been shamed, as noted in chapter 2, it is likely that they changed in spite of the shaming, rather than because of it. Furthermore, many of us assume that there's an inverse relationship between power and vulnerability—that the more power someone has, the less vulnerable they are to feeling shame. This is often not the case, and sometimes the opposite is true. Often, critics who publicly shame celebrities, and employees who talk degradingly about their supervisors, do so because they assume that the power-holders are somehow immune to such attacks. However, just about nobody is immune to the toxic and debilitating effects of shame; "punching up" nevertheless may deliver a harmful blow.

Another reason for the widespread use of shaming communi-cation is that the ethos of the culture in which the communication takes place (particularly in the US, but also in many places around the world, as most communication transpires online) has become such that we not only tolerate, but celebrate moral righteousness and the powerarchical attitudes and behaviors that accompany it. Indeed, we have learned to embrace a moral perfectionism whereby we hold others (and sometimes ourselves) to impossible standards: someone makes one unexamined—or even selfish—choice or state-ment and they become the enemy, the morally inferior *other*. We rally around those who raise the battle cry of moral righteousness and who are wielding power over others even as they call for justice and compassion, because we've learned to believe that abuse isn't really abuse as long as we're operating from a place of moral outrage. Moral righteousness can be intoxicating, as it has an addictive pull. So we must be vigilant in our efforts not to be seduced by its siren song. We must develop the self-awareness—the presence—that would enable us to notice and resist its attraction.

Being Present and Honoring Dignity

As we discussed in chapters 2 and 7, when we're more present, we're more connected—with ourselves and others. We're more spacious, better able to appreciate nuance and to sense and honor the dig-nity of others, even as we hold them accountable and seek to change problematic attitudes and behaviors. We recognize that good people can participate in harmful behaviors and that individuals are more than just their privilege. When we're more present, we're less hijacked by our painful feelings—we may feel them, but we recognize them for what they are: emotions that are a normal reaction to witnessing and being harmed by injustice. We don't mistake our feelings for ourselves, and we don't allow our feelings to create a narrative in which we see people as either perpetrators, victims, or heroes, with no overlap and no shades of gray. In other words, we feel and honor our emotions, but we don't let them override our recognition of our shared humanity.

In order to relate from a place of presence, timing matters. Everybody needs time to process painful emotions before being able to fully engage with those who have contributed to their suffering. We can know we're in a state of presence when we can feel and honor and even express our anger and grief without allowing these emotions to shape our narrative or drive our behaviors—when we can recognize the injustice caused by privilege, but we don't see the privileged individuals as morally inferior, and we don't feel the emotional charge of contempt.

This is not to suggest, as noted previously, that the responsibility for communicating effectively should be on the shoulders of those who are already carrying the burdens of injustice and suffering caused by privilege. Nor is it to suggest that we can, or should, remain silent until we're no longer angry. Especially for women, who have been socialized to deny and repress their anger—particularly anger toward patriarchy—it's important to reclaim this emotion. It is simply to suggest that we be mindful of our internal state and consider both the effectiveness and the appropriateness of our communications, which will make us more likely to bring about the kind of change we seek.

If our efforts to bring about positive change are driven by unprocessed pain, and especially trauma, we risk becoming, and creating, that which we seek to transform. We can see some of this (such as using all capital letters and multiple exclamation points). Powerarchical communication is epidemic in large part because the people propagating it are not held accountable, often because we believe that their ends (e.g., social justice) justify their means. Be extremely skeptical of anyone who claims that it's ever appropriate to communicate without compassion and respect. By its very nature, powerarchy seeks to perpetuate itself, and it continually constructs new and often elusive justifications toward this goal. One way to recognize powerarchical thinking in yourself is to ask yourself whether you're perceiving another as morally inferior and whether you're feeling the corresponding emotion of contempt.

When feasible, communicate with an individual privately, rather than in public. Of course, there are times when publicly pointing out someone's privileged behavior can be useful—such as when the person is a celebrity and is not personally accessible, or when it's important to publicly counter a problematic message they're communicating, or when they've engaged in bullying or violent behavior such as sexual harassment and they pose a threat to others. However, many people who make offensive statements are simply unaware of their privilege and end up being publicly reprimanded, when sharing critical feedback in private would be both more respectful and likely more strategic, as it doesn't make us come across as insensitive. Regardless of whether you're giving feedback privately or publicly, it's important to communicate respectfully.

Stay connected with your empathy. Imagine that the person with or about whom you're communicating is reading what you write or hearing what you say, and frame your message so that it honors their dignity, even as you point out the problems their privilege causes. (If you feel unsafe remaining empathic, worrying that you'll lose your own perspective if you're too open to the other's, then you might need more time to heal and shore up your psychological boundaries before speaking out about the issue.)

problematic communication when bullying, such as character assaults and shaming, is used to show that bullying is wrong. If we are not mindful of our approach to challenging privilege, we may, instead of creating a forum for collective healing and a just redistribution of power, simply feed the trauma of our base of supporters, reinforcing the very problem we're trying to resolve. We can, as noted previously, end up merely inverting the ladder of powerarchy, positioning a new group on the top of the same destructive hierarchy of moral worth.

Calling In and Creating Allies

When we "call in," as blogger Ngoc Loan Tran refers to it, rather than "call out," we invite others to be a part of the solution even if they're not fully engaged with the cause we're advocating.[12] Perhaps most notably, we work to raise awareness of oppressive behaviors without shaming; we hold others accountable and still treat them in a way that honors their dignity.

Calling in is not only a reflection of power with; it's also strategic. In democratic societies, social change is brought about not simply by a small group of core advocates who drive a countersystem but by a critical mass of supporters who help tip the scales of power. To attract popular support, advocates' messaging and interactions cannot be seen as "against" those whose support they wish to attract.

When we call in, we create allies. We give others the opportunity to be a part of the solution even if they don't follow all the tenets of our cause. For example, vegans can choose not to buy into the myth that one is either vegan and part of the solution, or not vegan and part of the problem. Vegans can appreciate that there is another option: someone can be a *vegan ally*, a nonvegan supporter of vegans and vegan values who uses their influence to help bring about the transformation of carnism. A vegan ally can, for example, stand up for vegans who are on the receiving end of hostile carnistic humor, speak out against carnism, or support vegan organizations and initiatives. And, ideally, they are being "as vegan as possible" when it comes to their own consumption.

Tips for Creating an Empowering Communicative Process

When the process of our communication is based on power with, our primary goal is to achieve mutual understanding rather than to "win" an argument, and our communication is empowering rather than shaming. So it's not enough for only the content of our communication to be based on power with (when, for instance, it's about social justice). If our communication is to be empowering, its process must reflect integrity and honor dignity. Following are some practical tips for creating an empowering communicative process that can increase the likelihood that our message will be heard and heeded.

Whenever possible, avoid absolutes. Absolutes are rarely accurate and come across as blaming all people for the behaviors of some. For example, instead of saying that "men" or "wealthy people" do something, say that "many men" or "some wealthy people" do it.

Don't assume that you know the internal experience of the privileged person(s) you're communicating with or about. Don't, for example, assume that you know why they said or did something insensitive—that they are "selfish" or "don't care"—or why they are motivated to ask questions ("He's using his male privilege to center himself"). Although it's important to think critically about the conversational dynamics around privilege and oppression, allowing others to be the experts on their own experience is a generosity we all deserve and is the opposite of the nonrelational attitude that reflects privilege.

Avoid character assassination. Calling someone a classist because they made a comment that's classist is conflating a person's character (which we can't know because we're not in their skin) with their behavior—and it's more likely to turn people off to a cause than to win supporters to it. So, for example, instead of saying, "You're a classist," you could say, "You made a statement that's classist."

Focus your communication on observable behaviors, not on your interpretations of the behaviors. For example, rather than say, "He made an ableist comment and won't respond to my criticism about it, so that means he wants to hold on to the power that comes with his privilege," simply focus on the comment and the fact that the person didn't respond. Moreover, be careful to examine your assumptions about what you perceive as privileged behavior. Try not to automatically assume that someone's powerholding position is to blame for problematic interactions, when other factors may be at play. For example, before assuming that male privilege is the reason your supervisor isn't acting on your recommendation, ask yourself if there may be other reasons for his decision. We must be mindful to approach difficult situations with as much objectivity as possible, lest we levy unfair accusations and perhaps avoid accountability for our own behaviors, thus limiting our personal and relational growth.

Stick to the facts. Avoid hyperbole and communicate the facts as objectively as possible. For example, don't refer to someone's comments that offended others as "malicious statements." We can't know the intention of another (unless they've told us), so we can't know if the statements were intended to harm. Instead, refer to such comments as "statements that were experienced as offensive."

Make sure that the facts you're communicating are accurate. There are countless examples on social media of comments that appear to reflect unexamined privilege or unethical behaviors but have been taken out of context or misconstrued and are accepted uncritically and disseminated unthinkingly. Such a lack of attentiveness can devastate the people whose words or actions are being publicly displayed, and creates fear and distrust in (sometimes millions of) onlookers.

Avoid sharing (or making) comments that are disrespectful or otherwise shaming. This includes comments that convey yelling

Speak to the person, not to their privilege, assuming good-will. It can help to remember that people are more than just their privilege, and that "good" people engage in harmful behaviors and that doesn't make them "bad." Believing that a person's engaging in problematic behavior means that they forfeit their right to be treated with basic respect is precisely the kind of thinking that caused the problem our communication is attempting to change.

Make sure the goal of your commentary is to raise awareness and bring about positive change, and ask yourself whether your communications are helping achieve this end. If your goal is to be right or to express your anger, your communication will no doubt reflect this fact and be unproductive or counterproductive. Of course, you *may* be right, and you may well have a right to be angry. It's simply important that these feelings not be ends in themselves.

• • •

When we appreciate the powerarchical mentality and dynamics that lie at the foundation of so much of the harm and suffering on our planet and understand how to work toward the alternative—a mentality and way of relating based on power with—we can more fully work together to create a world in which, as Carol J. Adams says, there are no "appropriate victims,"[13] exploited groups whose victimization is normalized and rendered invisible by their lower position on the hierarchy of moral worth. We can practice integrity and power with in our daily lives and in our work for social transformation. And in so doing, we can bring about the deep and broad transformation needed to shift from the epidemic relational pathology of powerarchy to the relational healing of power with.

The tools for such transformation lie within us. Research has shown that we are hardwired to empathize with others,[14] so in many ways, empathy is our natural state. We therefore don't have to learn how to care as much as unlearn how not to care. We simply need to more fully access our authentic selves—to reconnect with the parts of ourselves that have been buried beneath the fear, anger, and shame of powerarchical conditioning. Thus the Golden Rule shifts from being an impossible ideal that's regularly violated to a practical reality that's consistently honored. As Desmond Tutu said, "We are each made for goodness, love and compassion. Our lives are transformed as much as the world is when we live with these truths."[15]

NOTES

Introduction

1. See, for example, Polish, Jennifer. "Decolonizing Veganism: On Resisting Vegan Whiteness and Racism." In *Critical Perspectives on Veganism*, edited by Jodey Castricano and Rasmus R. Simonsen, 373–91. Palgrave Macmillan Animal Ethics Series. London: Palgrave Macmillan, Cham. doi:10.1007/978-3-319-33419-6_17; Harper, Breeze. *Sistah Vegan: Black Female Vegans Speak on Food, Identity, Health, and Society*. New York: Lantern, 2009; McQuirter, Tracye Lynn. *By Any Greens Necessary: A Revolutionary Guide for Black Women Who Want to Eat Great, Get Healthy, Lose Weight, and Look Phat*. Chicago: Chicago Review Press, 2010.

2. The same relational dynamics that enable oppression—the unjust use of power in a system in which there is an inequality of power and privilege between social groups—also enable abuse, which is the unjust use of power that is wielded against those who are not (necessarily) members of disenfranchised groups and that is often carried out on the interpersonal (or sometimes intrapersonal) level. This point is discussed further in chapter 2.

3. I acknowledge that oppression is a social, external phenomenon; however, I also believe that if we wish to transform oppression, we need to recognize how oppressive dynamics are also carried out on the other relational dimensions.

4. The perspective I bring to this book inevitably reflects those of the various groups—privileged and disadvantaged—to which I belong. I understand that as a white, able-bodied, cisgender woman, I cannot fully appreciate the experiences of members of the groups of which I am not a member.

5. See, for a small sample, such seminal works as Freire, Paulo. *Pedagogy of the Oppressed*. New York: Continuum, 2000. First published 1970;

Fanon, Frantz. *The Wretched of the Earth*. New York: Grove Press, 1963; hooks, bell. *Ain't I a Woman: Black Women and Feminism*. New York: Routledge, 2015. First published 1981; Lifton, Jay. *The Genocidal Mentality: Nazi Holocaust and Nuclear Threat*. London: Macmillan, 1991; and, more recently, Alexander, Michelle. *The New Jim Crow: Mass Incarceration in the Age of Colorblindness*. New York: New Press, 2011.

6. After writing this book, I discovered the term *powerarchy* in Makhoul, Saná. "Unveiling North African Women, Revisited: An Arab Feminist Critique of Orientalist Mentality in Visual Art and Ethnography." *Anthropology of Consciousness* 9 (1998): 39–48. doi:10.1525/ac.1998.9.4.39. Makhoul uses the term to describe not the dynamic operations of systemic oppressions but, rather, dyadic power relations that are abstracted from psychological relationship. I further discovered the term in the writing of blogger mdkberry, who uses it to mischaracterize women as having "always been the arbiters of society" (mdkberry, "Powerarchy: Women Have Always Been the Arbiters of Society," https://steemit.com/patriarchy/@mdkberry/powerarchy-women-have-always-been-the-arbiters-of-society) (Steemit, 2017). Powerarchy is a concept that in some ways builds on Gramsci's notion of cultural hegemony. Like cultural hegemony, powerarchy is an entrenched system of domination. The key ways powerarchy differs from cultural hegemony are that powerarchy applies not only to social relations but also to psychological dynamics, and it is not limited to interactions among humans, as it includes human interactions with nonhuman beings and the environment. Gramsci's concept of cultural hegemony is primarily explored in Gramsci, Antonio. *Prison Notebooks*, Volumes 1–3. Edited and translated by J. A. Buttigieg and A. Callari. New York: Columbia University Press, 2011.

7. Relational-Cultural Theory recognizes the existence of relational power. It places an emphasis on the exercise of joint power or "power with," rather than "power over" others, as a way of promoting mutual growth and development (see Miller, Jean Baker, and Irene Pierce Stiver. *The Healing Connection: How Women Form Relationships in Therapy and in Life*. Boston: Beacon Press, 1997; Surrey, Janet L. "Relationship and Empowerment." In *Women's Growth in Connection: Writings from the Stone Center*, edited by Judith V. Jordan, Alexandra G. Kaplan,

Irene P. Stiver, Janet L. Surrey, and Jean Baker Miller. New York: Guilford Press, 1991; and West, Carolyn K. "The Map of Relational-Cultural Theory." *Women & Therapy* 28, no. 3–4 (2005): 93–110, doi: 10.1300/J015v28n03_05). This requires an acknowledgment of and commitment to relational interdependence, collective learning, and mutual empowerment and engagement (see, for example, Fletcher, J. "The Paradox of Post-heroic Leadership: An Essay on Gender, Power and Transformational Change." *Leadership Quarterly* 15 (2004): 647–61, doi:10.1016/j.leaqua.2004.07.004; and Fletcher, Joyce K., and Katrin Käufer. "Shared Leadership: Paradox and Possibility." In *Shared Leadership: Reframing the Hows and Whys of Leadership,* edited by Craig L. Pearce and Jay A. Conger. Thousand Oaks: Sage Publications, 2003). "Global Wealth Databook 2015." *Credit Suisse—Research Institute,* October 2015. http://delangemars.nl/wp-content/uploads/2015/10/global-wealth-databook-20151.pdf; Mujcic, Redzo, and Paul Frijters. "Still Not Allowed on the Bus: It Matters If You're Black or White!" *Forschungsinstitut zur Zukunft der Arbeit.* Discussion Paper No. 7300, March 2013. http://ftp.iza.org/dp7300.pdf.

Chapter 1

1. There is, of course, also significant suffering inherent in nature, such as that of wild animal populations that are not impacted by humans.
2. The same dynamics that underlie oppressive behavior toward others also underlie self-destructive behaviors.
3. Associated Press. "U.S. Court Rules Jews Are Protected 'Race' under Civil Rights Act of 1964." *Haaretz,* July 19, 2018. https://www.haaretz.com/us-news/u-s-court-rules-jews-are-protected-race-under-civil-rights-act-1.6291921. See also US Senate Committee of Health, Education, Labor and Pensions. Anti-Semitism Awareness Act of 2018. S. 2940, 11th Cong., 2nd sess. https://www.congress.gov/115/bills/s2940/BILLS-115s2940is.xml.
4. White House. Protecting the Nation from Foreign Terrorist Entry into the United States. Executive order 13780 (January 27, 2017). *Federal Register* 82, no. 20 (February 15, 2017): 8977–82. https://www.whitehouse.gov/presidential-actions/executive-order-protecting-nation-foreign-terrorist-entry-united-states/. See also *Supreme Court*

of the United States: Trump, President of the United States, et al. v. Hawaii et al. (No. 17-965, June 26, 2018). www.supremecourt.gov /search.aspx?search=Trump+vs.+Hawaii&type=Site.

5. Carson, E. Ann. *Prisoners in 2016.* Bureau of Justice Statistics, US Department of Justice, Office of Justice Programs. August 7, 2018. https://www.bjs.gov/content/pub/pdf/p16.pdf. See also Alexander, Michelle. *The New Jim Crow: Mass Incarceration in the Age of Color-blindness.* New York: New Press, 2011; and Duvernay, Ava (director). *13th.* 2016. Netflix. https://www.netflix.com/de/title/80091741.

6. Some scholars suggest that racism is the foundation of some other forms of oppression. See, for example, Ko, Aph, and Syl Ko. *Aphro-ism: Essays on Pop Culture, Feminism, and Black Veganism from Two Sisters.* New York: Lantern Books, 2017.

7. Kimberle Crenshaw has done vitally important work illuminating how oppressions intersect and what this means for social justice. See Crenshaw, Kimberle. "Demarginalizing the Intersection of Race and Sex: A Black Feminist Critique of Antidiscrimination Doctrine, Feminist Theory and Antiracist Politics." *University of Chicago Legal Forum* no. 1(1989): art. 8. http://chicagounbound.uchicago.edu/uclf /vol1989/iss1/8.

8. The most comprehensive research on moral values was conducted by Jonathan Haidt and Jesse Grahm, which served as the basis of their moral foundations theory. Haidt and Grahm found that five moral values are shared across cultures, and that two of those values—caring and fairness (compassion and justice)—are most equitably espoused by all individuals. For more on moral foundations theory, see moralfoundations.org and Haidt, Jonathan. *The Righteous Mind: Why Good People Are Divided by Politics and Religion.* New York: Pantheon Books, 2012.

9. Tasca, Cecilia, Mariangela Rapetti, Mauro Giovanni Carta, and Bianca Fadda. "Women and Hysteria in the History of Mental Health." *Clinical Practice and Epidemiology in Mental Health* 8 (2012): 110–19.

10. I understand that the terms *male* and *female* reflect gender binarism, and I have avoided using them as much as possible. I have only used these terms when they've been necessary to accurately communicate a concept. I have also chosen to use the singular plural (*they, their,* and so forth) in order to avoid language that reflects gender binarism.

11. Hicks, Donna. *Dignity: The Essential Role It Plays in Resolving Conflict.* New Haven, CT: Yale University Press, 2011.

12. Many philosophers have explored how to determine whether an individual is deserving of moral consideration: What, they ask, should be the defining criterion? Most philosophers today agree that all human beings deserve moral consideration—though such consideration may be forfeited through one's subsequent actions or inactions. More controversial has been whether nonhuman animals should be included in the sphere of moral consideration. Peter Singer suggests that the defining criterion for moral consideration is *sentience*, the capacity to feel pleasure and pain. And because nonhuman animals, like human animals, are sentient—that is, they have feelings and are vulnerable to harm—they deserve moral consideration of their interests. Tom Regan suggests that the criterion for moral consideration is being a "subject of a life," which includes self-consciousness, emotions, and certain types of cognitive processes. Thus Regan also argues that nonhuman animals must be included in the sphere of moral consideration. For more information on this issue, see Singer, Peter. *Animal Liberation: A New Ethics for Our Treatment of Animals.* New York: New York Review, 1975; and Regan, Tom. *The Case for Animal Rights.* Berkeley: University of California Press, 2004. First published 1983.

13. I am not suggesting that plants and animals have the same interests but rather that the ecosystems that are homes for nonhuman animals and that comprise living flora should be included in the sphere of moral consideration. Our current course of ecological devastation reflects precisely what happens when we don't consider the interests of ecosystems.

14. See, for example, David, E.J.R., and Annie O. Derthick. *The Psychology of Oppression.* New York: Springer, 2017; Guinote, Ana, and Theresa K. Vescio, eds. *The Social Psychology of Power.* New York: Guilford Press, 2010; Prilleltensky, Isaac, and Dennis R. Fox. "Psychopolitical Literacy for Wellness and Justice." *Journal of Community Psychology* 35, no. 6 (2007): 793–805; Oliver, Kelly. *The Colonization of Psychic Space: A Psychoanalytic Social Theory of Oppression.* Minneapolis: University of Minnesota Press, 2004; Miller, Jean Baker. *Toward a New Psychology of Women.* Boston: Beacon Press, 1987. First

published 1976; and Fanon, Frantz. *The Wretched of the Earth*. New York: Grove Press, 1963.

15. Hicks, *Dignity.*

16. This trend is fortunately changing. Some notable works examining the role of psychology in enabling oppression include David and Derthick, *Psychology of Oppression*; Ratner, Carl. *Macro Cultural Psychology: A Political Philosophy of Mind*. New York: Oxford University Press, 2012; Guinote and Vescio, *Social Psychology of Power*; Fox, Dennis, Isaac Prilleltensky, and Stephanie Austin, eds. *Critical Psychology: An Introduction*, 2nd ed. Thousand Oaks, CA: Sage, 2009; Oliver, *Colonization of Psychic Space*; Miller, *Toward a New Psychology of Women*; Fanon, *Wretched of the Earth*; and Fromm, Erich. *The Pathology of Normalcy*. New York: American Mental Health Foundation Books, 2010. First published 1953.

17. Ko and Ko, *Aphro-ism.*

18. See, for example, the work of John Gottman and Julie Schwartz Gottman at https://www.gottman.com/.

19. The relational behaviors I discuss in this book draw and expand on those described in RCT and include the key elements necessary for fostering secure attachment.

20. See Ainsworth, Mary D. Salter. "Attachments and Other Affectional Bonds across the Life Cycle." In *Attachment across the Life Cycle*, edited by Colin Murray Parkes, Joan Stevenson-Hinde, and Peter Marris, 33–51. London: Routledge, 1991; Bowlby, John. *Attachment and Loss*. Vol. 1, *Attachment*, 2nd ed. New York: Basic Books, 1982. First published 1969.

21. Practicing integrity—acting in alignment with core moral values such as compassion, justice, and honesty—is essential for creating connection, security, and empowerment. In order for someone to feel connected, secure, and empowered within a relational dynamic, they must trust that the other with whom they are relating will treat them with kindness and will be fair and truthful.

22. See, for example, Banks, Amy, and Leigh Ann Hirschman. *Wired to Connect: The Surprising Link between Brain Science and Strong, Healthy Relationships*. New York: TarcherPerigee, 2016; Jordan, Judith V., ed. *The Power of Connection: Recent Developments in Relational-Cultural Theory*. New York: Routledge, 2010; and Tatkin, Stan. *Wired for Love:*

How Understanding Your Partner's Brain and Attachment Style Can Help You Defuse Conflict and Build a Secure Relationship. Oakland, CA: New Harbinger, 2012.

23. For an excellent overview of attachment styles and how they impact relational dynamics, see Levine, Amir, and Rachel S. F. Heller. *Attached: The New Science of Adult Attachment and How It Can Help You Find—and Keep—Love*. New York: TarcherPerigee, 2010.

24. See Ainsworth, "Attachments."

25. Research on the influence of systems on attachment styles could yield important information regarding what kinds of political, economic, and other institutions promote or hinder social well-being.

26. Sometimes people in a relationship start out with equal amounts of power, but the abusive dynamic creates an imbalance.

27. See Bancroft, Lundy. *Why Does He Do That? Inside the Minds of Angry and Controlling Men*. New York: Berkeley Books, 2002.

28. For a history of the role of institutionalized patriarchy in normalizing domestic violence, see Dobash, R. Emerson, and Russell Dobash. *Violence against Wives: A Case against the Patriarchy*. New York: Free Press, 1979. For a more recent discussion of the use of patriarchy as a model for understanding domestic violence, see Hunnicutt, Gwen. "Varieties of Patriarchy and Violence against Women: Resurrecting 'Patriarchy' as a Theoretical Tool." *Violence against Women* 15, no. 5 (2009): 553–73. https://doi.org/10.1177 /1077801208331246.

29. I am including in the collective dimension how we relate to nonhuman animals and the environment.

30. I am not suggesting that oppression is not a deeply entrenched, institutionalized reality that is maintained by powerful social structures, but rather that examining these structures through a relational lens can help deepen our understanding of oppressive dynamics.

31. I am aware that some of the key relational constructs I refer to, such as power and shame, reflect a Western view of relationships and that more research is needed examining how such constructs are understood and experienced cross-culturally. However, some research suggests considerable consistency in how these phenomena are experienced across cultures. See, for example, Sznycer, Daniel, John Tooby, Leda Cosmides, Roni Porat, Shaul Shalvi, and Eran Halperin.

"Shame Closely Tracks the Threat of Devaluation by Others, Even across Cultures." *Proceedings of the National Academy of Sciences*, February 22, 2016. doi:10.1073/pnas.1514699113.

Chapter 2

1. This statement is frequently attributed to both Adolf Hitler and Joseph Goebbels. It appears to derive from Hitler's discussion, in *Mein Kampf*, of a propaganda technique he associates with Jews and Marxists.
2. This quote appears in print in the screenplay of *Gandhi* (1982) by John Briley. Briley, John. *Gandhi: The Screenplay*. London: Duckworth, 1982. https://www.weeklyscript.com/Gandhi.html. The passage subsequently appears in Ronald Reagan's address to the United Nations General Assembly on September 24, 1984. See "Transcript of Reagan's Address to the U.N. General Assembly." *New York Times Archives*, September 25, 1984. https://www.nytimes.com/1984/09/25/world/transcript-of-reagan-s-address-to-the-un-general-assembly.html?pagewanted=all.
3. For a detailed discussion of various forms of power, see Guinote, Ana, and Theresa K. Vescio, eds. *The Social Psychology of Power*. New York: Guilford Press, 2010.
4. I use *powerful* in the technical sense of the term, to denote either being or feeling "full" of power—having or believing one has the ability to act or influence. I also use *powerful* (as a feeling) to describe the "high" that has been shown to correlate with this feeling, which reflects an increase in dopamine and has led some researchers to suggest that power is addictive. (I am operating under the assumption that feeling powerful exists on a spectrum, and the corresponding high emerges when one has a sufficient level of this feeling.) So feeling "powerful" can mean feeling one has the power to act, and/or the feeling of high one gets from having a certain amount of power.
5. I use *empowered* and *feeling empowered* to denote having the ability to act or influence or to denote the feeling a person has when they have such ability. Although *powerful* and *empowered* are synonymous when it comes to one meaning—having the ability to act or influence or the feeling of having such an ability—there are two differences in how these terms may be interpreted. First, feeling powerful is often (though not always) a comparative experience, meaning that a person

may feel more or less powerful based on how their level of power compares to that of another, whereas one tends to feel empowered (or not) regardless of whether or not others are empowered. Second, although the feeling of being powerful has been shown to correlate with an increase in dopamine, it appears that no similar studies have been done on the neurochemistry of empowerment, and I am operating under the assumption that feeling empowered does not entail a high.

6. For a comprehensive discussion of self-perception and psychosocial functioning, see Bandura, Albert. *Self-Efficacy: The Exercise of Self-Control.* New York: W.H. Freedman and Company, 1997.

7. The process of an interaction often reflects the purpose. For instance, the way we use power (the process), such as abusing it rather than respecting it, is often because we want to harm or control another (the purpose). Sometimes, however, the process and the purpose differ. For example, perhaps we abuse power not in order to negatively impact another or others but because we don't care about our impact on them, as when we purchase a high-emissions vehicle that we know causes damage to the environment. Or, in certain cases, we're simply not aware that we're abusing power when we're doing so. Regardless of our motivation, the process we use can cause harm, and it is primarily on the level of process that powerarchy is maintained and can be transformed.

8. One of the most notable researchers examining the intersection of power, prejudice, social cognition, and stereotypes is Susan Fiske. See, for example, Fiske, S. T. "Controlling Other People: The Impact of Power on Stereotyping." *American Psychologist* 48, no. 6 (1993): 621–28. http://dx.doi.org/10.1037/0003-066X.48.6.621.

9. I do not mean to oversimplify the complex issue of power models and power dynamics. I do not provide a more nuanced analysis because the purpose of this book is not to examine the intricacies of power structures but to give an overview of power models simply as they relate to powerarchy.

10. I use *disempowerment* to denote either a state of lacking the agency to act or influence, or a feeling of such a lack. In other words, a person can *be* disempowered (lacking agency), or they can *feel* disempowered (lacking belief in agency that they actually have).

11. Breakthrough studies in neuroscience have shown that we are actually hardwired for connection—that we are fundamentally relational beings who strive for connection and seek to avoid the pain of disconnection just as we seek to avoid physical pain. Data also shows that the brain grows in connection. See, for example, Gerhardt, Sue. *Why Love Matters: How Affection Shapes a Baby's Brain.* Hove, East Sussex, UK: Brunner-Routledge, 2004.

12. For more information on the functionalist model, see Overbeck, Jennifer R. "Concepts and Historical Perspectives on Power." In *Social Psychology of Power*, edited by Guinote and Vescio, 19–45.

13. The power models I describe here are based on the dominance and functionalist models noted in the social science literature, and they include the concepts provided by Mary Parker Follett, who coined the terms *power over* and *power with* to describe distinct models of power. They also include the conceptual model of Kenneth Boulding, who built on Follett's analysis and described "threat," "exchange," and "love" as forms of power, and that of Jean Baker Miller, who put forth a relational model of power. I have slightly modified the functionalist/power-with model to reflect a synthesis and extended analysis of the corresponding theories. See Follet, Mary P. *Dynamic Administration: The Collected Papers of Mary Parker Follet*, edited by E. M. Fox and L. Urwick. London: Pitman Publishing, 1940; Boulding, Kenneth E. *Three Faces of Power.* Newbury Park, CA: Sage Publications, 1989; and Miller, Jean B. *Toward a New Psychology of Women.* Boston: Beacon Press, 1987.

14. I differentiate a behavior, which is a singular action, from a dynamic, which is an interaction (involving two or more behaviors).

15. Tracy, Jessica L., and Robins, Richard W. "Death of a (Narcissistic) Salesman: An Integrative Model of Fragile Self-Esteem: Comment." *Psychological Inquiry* 14, no. 1 (2003): 57–62.

16. Although culture plays a significant role in determining what qualities we define as affording one power, individual subjectivity also plays a role. For example, even if we live in a culture that largely conflates beauty and power, we may not personally afford beauty such status. So, even though we'll still be heavily influenced by the broader culture, we may nevertheless afford beauty less status than someone whose personal values coincide more fully with those of the culture.

17. For an insightful reflection on otherness as a basis for subjugation, see Morrison, Toni. *The Origin of Others.* Cambridge, MA: Harvard University Press, 2017.

18. Shafer, Carolyn M., and Marilyn Frye. "Rape and Respect." In *Feminism and Philosophy*, edited by Mary Vetterling-Braggin, Frederick A. Elliston, and Jane English, 333–46. Savage, MD: Rowman & Littlefield, 1977.

19. Bloom, Sandra L., and Brian Farragher. "Authoritarianism, Learned Helplessness, and Disempowerment." In *Destroying Sanctuary: The Crisis in Human Service Delivery Systems.* New York: Oxford University Press, 2011; Young, Judith H. "Psychological Control: States of Mental Disempowerment." *Global Research*, October 25, 2008. https://www.globalresearch.ca/psychological-control-states-of -mental-disempowerment/10687.

20. Singer, Margaret T. "Therapy with Ex-Cult Members." *Journal of the National Association of Private Psychiatric Hospitals* 9, no. 4 (1978): 14–18; Clark, John G., Jr. "Cults." *Journal of the American Medical Association* 242, no. 3 (1979): 279–81. doi:10.1001/jama.1979.033 00030051026.

21. Carballo, David M., Paul Roscoe, and Gary M. Feinman. "Cooperation and Collective Action in the Cultural Evolution of Complex Societies." *Journal of Archaeological Method and Theory* 21, no. 1 (March 2014): 98–133.

22. When I refer to empowerment throughout this book, I am referring to "relational" empowerment—behaviors that empower individuals to act in relationally healthful ways.

23. Strohminger, Nina, and Shaun Nichols. "The Essential Moral Self." *Cognition—International Journal of Cognitive Science* 131, no. 1 (2014): 159–171.

24. Peck, M. Scott. *The Road Less Traveled: A New Psychology of Love, Traditional Values, and Spiritual Growth.* New York: Simon & Schuster, 1978.

25. See Tolle, Eckhart. *The Power of Now: A Guide to Spiritual Enlightenment.* Novato, CA: New World Library, 1999.

26. See Scheff, Thomas J., and Suzanne M. Retzinger. *Emotions and Violence: Shame and Rage in Destructive Conflicts.* Self-published, iUniverse, 2001; and Hicks, Donna. *Dignity: The Essential Role It Plays in Resolving Conflict.* New Haven, CT: Yale University Press, 2011.

27. Of course, in and of themselves, these behaviors don't necessarily mean we are compensating for shame; the determining factor is our motivation for them.
28. See Hicks, *Dignity.*
29. Different individuals respond to traumatizing events in different ways; here, I describe the common denominators that cause traumatization in most people.
30. There are a variety of reasons for trauma being so disconnecting; for an excellent resource, see Herman, Judith. *Trauma and Recovery: The Aftermath of Violence—From Domestic Abuse to Political Terror.* New York: Basic Books, 1997.

Chapter 3

1. See Lerner, Harriet. *The Dance of Connection.* New York: William Morrow Paperbacks, 2002.
2. See Schwartz, Richard C. *Introduction to the Internal Family Systems Model.* Oak Park, IL: Trailheads Publications, 2001.
3. Lerner, Harriet. *The Dance of Intimacy.* New York: HarperCollins, 1989.
4. Of course, the sexual objectification of women was not a new phenomenon; it simply became more overt and infused in women's gender identity.
5. As noted in chapter 2, power-over dynamics are the dynamics of addiction and trauma. Interestingly, psychologist Anne Wilson Schaef and organizational consultant Diane Fassel observed that in families where one or more members suffer from addiction, the whole family system can take on the personality and behaviors of an addicted individual. Schaef and Fassel named such systems "addictive systems," describing them as closed systems that are organized around maintaining the defensive mentality and behaviors of addiction. More recent examinations of family systems have shown that it's actually not necessary for an addicted individual to be present for the dynamics of an addictive system to exist; similar dynamics have been found in families where trauma and other forms of relational dysfunction have been present. It's important to note that family systems where addiction or trauma are present need not necessarily become powerarchies, and also that, when they do, it is not an indicator that the members

don't care about one another or are not trying to resolve the problem. In many powerarchical family systems, members are simply coping with difficulties the best way they know how. See Schaef, Anne Wilson, and Diane Fassel. *The Addictive Organization: Why We Overwork, Cover Up, Pick Up the Pieces, Please the Boss, and Perpetuate Sick Organizations*. San Francisco: HarperOne, 1990; Schaef, Anne Wilson. *When Society Becomes an Addict*. San Francisco: HarperSanFrancisco, 1987.

6. Allan G. Johnson describes what he calls "systems of privilege" in his excellent text *Privilege, Power, and Difference*. Social powerarchies are similar to systems of privilege, but with dimensions that extend beyond what Johnson describes in his work. Johnson, Allan G. *Privilege, Power, and Difference*. New York: McGraw-Hill Education, 2005.

7. See Eisler, Riane. *The Chalice and the Blade: Our History, Our Future*. San Francisco: HarperOne, 2011.

8. Patricia Hill Collins suggests that there is a "matrix of domination" in which people are placed in categories based on such criteria as race, class, and sexual orientation and then are judged as deviant and inferior when measured against the qualities and values of the dominant group. Collins, Patricia Hill. *Black Feminist Thought: Knowledge, Consciousness, and the Politics of Empowerment*. Boston: Unwin Hyman, 1990.

9. Feminist theologian Elisabeth Schüssler Fiorenza proposed the concept of *kyriarchy*, a system of domination similar to patriarchy but that extends beyond gender. Kyriarchy, however, does not account for human–nonhuman relations (nonhuman animals, the environment), nor is it based on a psychological framework, so I have not used it as the basis of my work here. As noted in chapter 1, some scholars suggest that racism forms the foundation of some other oppressions. See, for example Ko, Aph, and Syl Ko. *Aphro-ism: Essays on Pop Culture, Feminism, and Black Veganism from Two Sisters*. New York: Lantern Books, 2017.

10. The notion of interlocking oppressions emerged in large part from the work of Kimberle Crenshaw, who introduced the concept of intersectionality. See Crenshaw, Kimberle. "Demarginalizing the Intersection of Race and Sex: A Black Feminist Critique of Antidiscrimination Doctrine, Feminist Theory and Antiracist Politics."

University of Chicago Legal Forum no. 1 (1989): art. 8. http://chicagounbound.uchicago.edu/uclf/vol1989/iss1/8.

11. See Butler, Robert, N. "Successful Aging and the Role of the Life Review." *Journal of the American Geriatrics Society* 22 (1974): 529–35. doi:10.1111/j.1532-5415.1974.tb04823.x. See also Applewhite, Ashton. *This Chair Rocks: A Manifesto against Ageism.* New York: Macmillan, 2019; Lamb, Sarah, ed. *Successful Aging as a Contemporary Obsession.* New Brunswick, NJ: Rutgers University Press, 2017.

12. Robbins-Ruszkowski, Jessica. "Aspiring to Activity: Universities of the Third Age, Gardening, and Other Forms of Living in Postsocialist Poland." In *Successful Aging,* edited by Lamb, 112–25.

13. See Lamb, *Successful Aging.*

14. I am describing binary groups to demonstrate how these groups are typically framed in a powerarchy, and I acknowledge that binaries are often social constructs.

15. The terms *majority* and *minority* were once used to describe members of dominant and nondominant groups, but such terms have been misconstrued. Although these terms refer to groups that hold the majority or minority of power, most people interpret them as referring to groups that make up more or less of the population.

16. US Census Bureau. "Population Estimates, July 1, 2016." https://www.census.gov/quickfacts/fact/table/US/PST045216.

17. Bialik, Kristen, and Jens Manual Krogstad. "115th Congress Sets New High for Racial, Ethnic Diversity." Pew Research Center, January 24, 2017. http://www.pewresearch.org/fact-tank/2017/01/24/115th-congress-sets-new-high-for-racial-ethnic-diversity/.

18. Kurtzleben, Danielle. "How the Donald Trump Cabinet Stacks Up, in 3 Charts." National Public Radio, December 28, 2016. https://www.npr.org/2016/12/28/506299885/how-the-donald-trump-cabinet-stacks-up-in-3-charts.

19. McConnell, Allen, and Jill Leibold. "Relations among the Implicit Association Test, Discriminatory Behavior, and Explicit Measures of Racial Attitudes." *Journal of Experimental Social Psychology* 37 (2001): 435–42. https://doi.org/10.1006/jesp.2000.1470; Mahzarin, Banaji, and Jerry Kang. "Fair Measures: A Behavioral Realist Revision of Affirmative Action." *California Law Review* 94 (2006). https://doi.org/10.15779/Z38370Q; Greenwald, Anthony, and Linda Krieger.

"Implicit Bias: Scientific Foundations." *California Law Review* 94, no. 4 (2006): 945–68. https://doi.org/10.15779/Z38GH7F.

20. She, Hsiao-Ching. "The Interplay of a Biology Teacher's Beliefs, Teaching Practices and Gender-Based Student-Teacher Classroom Interaction." *Educational Research* 42, no. 1 (2000): 100–11, doi: 10.1080/001318800363953; McClowry, Sandra. "Teacher/Student Interactions and Classroom Behavior: The Role of Student Temperament and Gender." *Journal of Research in Childhood Education* 27, no. 3 (2013). doi: 10.1080/02568543.2013.796330.

21. Johnson, *Privilege*.

22. Even when powerholders are conscious of the controlling tactics they use in powerarchical relationships, the nonpowerholders are usually not aware of the roles and rules that maintain the powerarchy.

23. These myths share some commonalities with, but are distinct from, the legitimizing myths that justify social dominance put forth by Jim Sidanius. See Sidanius, Jim, Erik Devereux, and Felicia Pratto. "A Comparison of Symbolic Racism Theory and Social Dominance Theory as Explanations for Racial Policy Attitude." *Journal of Social Psychology* 132, no. 3 (1992): 377–95.

24. Cognitive distortions are commonly referred to as "psychological defense mechanisms," and in my other writings I use this more common phrase. However, in this book I use the term *cognitive distortions* to avoid confusing readers by using "defense" to describe one of three defenses.

Chapter 4

1. This paragraph was first published in Joy, Melanie. *Beyond Beliefs: A Guide to Improving Relationships and Communication for Vegans, Vegetarians, and Meateaters.* New York: Lantern Books, 2018.

2. Kowol, Adam. "The Theory of Cognitive Dissonance." Personal website of Adam Kowol, 2008. http://adamkowol.info/works/Festinger .pdf; Breslavs, Gershon M. "Moral Emotions, Conscience, and Cognitive Dissonance." *Psychology of Thinking* 6, no. 4 (2013): 65–72.

3. See Festinger, Leon. *A Theory of Cognitive Dissonance.* Stanford, CA: Stanford University Press, 1957.

4. For more information on carnism, see Joy, Melanie. *Why We Love Dogs, Eat Pigs, and Wear Cows: An Introduction to Carnism.* Newburyport,

MA: Conari Press, 2011; and Joy, Melanie. "Beyond Carnism and Toward Rational, Authentic Food Choices." TEDx. February 5, 2015. https://www.youtube.com/watch?v=o0VrZPBskpg. Available at https://www.carnism.org.

5. Many of the defenses in this chapter apply to interpersonal powerarchies as well.

6. I acknowledge that there are many individuals who are not in a position to make their food choices freely, such as those who are economically disadvantaged or are geographically unable to access a variety of foods.

7. See Hedges, Chris. *What Every Person Should Know about War.* New York: Free Press, 2003; and "FAOSTAT: Livestock Primary." Food and Agriculture Organization of the United Nations, 2017, http://www.fao.org/faostat/en/#data/QL.

8. The small percentage of farmed animals that are "humanely" raised also suffer intensely. Many of these individuals are raised in similar circumstances to those in factory farms, and virtually all of them are ultimately sent to the same slaughterhouses that are used for factory-farmed animals.

9. Dawkins, Marian. "The Science of Animal Suffering." *Ethology* 114, no. 10 (2008): 937–45. doi:10.1111/j.1439-0310.2008.01557.x.

10. Toobin, Jeffrey. "The Facts in the Zimmerman Trial." *New Yorker*, July 2013. https://www.newyorker.com/news/daily-comment/the-facts-in-the-zimmerman-trial; Alvarez, Lizette. "In Zimmerman Case, Self-Defense Was Hard to Topple." *New York Times*, July 2013. http://www.nytimes.com/2013/07/15/us/in-zimmerman-case-self-defense-was-hard-to-topple.html.

11. Beer, Todd. "Police Killings of Blacks: Data for 2015, 2016, 2017." *Society Pages*, 2018. https://thesocietypages.org/toolbox/police-killing-of-blacks/.

12. For an overview of the politics of police killings of people of color in the United States, see Martinot, Steve. "On the Epidemic of Police Killings" *Social Justice* 39, no. 4 (2014): 52–75.

13. A cisgender individual has an identity (e.g., male or female) that corresponds to their birth sex. If we are gender conforming, we behave in ways that conform with gender expectations. So, for example, if we're a man, we wear pants rather than skirts, and if we're a woman, we shave our legs.

14. Although in much of the world stoning women is no longer practiced, in some places it is still acceptable.
15. In some societies and languages, it is still normal to use the term *invalid.*
16. Although in some societies significant improvements have been made to meet the needs of individuals who have disabilities, there is still much progress to be made to truly meet their needs and respect their rights.
17. See Fine, Cordelia. "The Most Neurosexist Study of the Year?" *Slate,* December 4, 2013. http://www.slate.com/articles/health_and_science /science/2013/12/hard_wired_brain_differences_critique_of_male _female_neuroscience_imaging.html; Fine, Cordelia. *Delusions of Gender: How Our Minds, Society, and Neurosexism Create Difference.* New York: Norton, 2010. See also the work of Dr. Anne Fausto-Sterling: see "Articles" on her website: http://www.annefaustosterling .com/articles/.
18. *Broadcasting Genocide: Censorship, Propaganda & State-Sponsored Violence in Rwanda 1990–1994.* Article 19, p. 67. https://www.article19 .org/data/files/pdfs/publications/rwanda-broadcasting-genocide .pdf.
19. "Goebbels Claims Jews Will Destroy Culture." Video. *Holocaust Encyclopedia.* United States Holocaust Memorial Museum. https:// encyclopedia.ushmm.org/content/en/film/goebbels-claims-jews-will -destroy-culture.
20. Disability rights activist Stella Young coined the phrase *inspiration porn* to describe media that sensationalizes people with disabilities, depicting them as inspirational solely or partly due to their disability. Grue, Jan. "The Problem with Inspiration Porn: A Tentative Definition and a Provisional Critique." *Disability & Society* 31, no. 6 (2016): 838–49. doi: 10.1080/09687599.2016.1205473.
21. Often the proponents of a countersystem are members of the nondominant group most impacted by the social powerarchy being challenged—for instance, many antiracism advocates are people of color. Other times, the proponents are not directly oppressed by the social powerarchy but are advocates for the victims, as with vegans. It's important to note, however, that even when advocates are not direct victims, they may still constitute a nondominant (and sometimes

marginalized) group within the social powerarchy. Vegans, for example, are ideological minorities. Although their minority status and experience are obviously quite different from those of, for instance, Muslims or women, they do experience certain forms of prejudice and discrimination, and when interacting with nonvegans (all other social power roles being equal), they are often on the lower end of an invisible power imbalance.

22. Hancock, Adrienne B., and Benjamin A. Rubin. "Influence of Communication Partner's Gender on Language." *Journal of Language and Society* 34, no. 1 (2015): 46–64.

23. James, Deborah, and Sandra Clarke. "Women, Men, and Interruptions." In *Gender and Conversational Interaction*, edited by Deborah Tannen. Oxford Studies in Sociolinguistics. Oxford: Oxford University Press, 1993, pp. 231–80.

24. See, for example, Vernasco, Lucy. "Seven Studies Proving Mansplaining Exists." *Bitchmedia*, July 14, 2014. https://www.bitchmedia.org /post/seven-studies-proving-mansplaining-exists.

25. "Understanding and Addressing Violence against Women: Intimate Partner Violence." World Health Organization and Pan American Health Organization, 2012. http://www.who.int/int/iris/handle /10665/77432.

26. In 2010, an average of twenty people every minute experienced intimate partner physical violence in the United States alone— amounting to more than ten million abuse victims per year. Black, Michele C., Kathleen C. Basile, Matthew J. Breiding, Sharon G. Smith, Mikel L. Walters, Melissa T. Merrick, Jieru Chen, and Mark R. Stevens. *National Intimate Partner and Sexual Violence Survey: 2010 Summary Report.* Atlanta, GA: National Center for Injury Prevention and Control, Centers for Disease Control and Prevention, 2010. http://www.cdc.gov/violenceprevention/pdf/nisvs _report2010-a.pdf.

27. Bancroft, Lundy. *Why Does He Do That? Inside the Minds of Angry and Controlling Men.* New York: Berkeley Books, 2002. See also Harris, Tal, Laurie B. Moret, Jerry Gale, and Karen L. Kampmeyer. "Therapists' Gender Assumptions and How These Assumptions Influence Therapy." *Journal of Feminist Family Therapy* 12, nos. 2–3 (2001): 33–59. doi:10.1300/J086v12n02_02.

28. Although projection sometimes involves projecting unconscious impulses or qualities onto another (or others), this section is not referring to projection in that strict Freudian sense of the term.

29. Lamb-Books, Benjamin. *Angry Abolitionists and the Rhetoric of Slavery—Moral Emotions in Social Movements.* London: Palgrave Macmillan, 2016.

30. "The Campaign for Women's Suffrage." *BBC KS3 Bitesize* (2014). https://www.bbc.com/bitesize/guides/zy2ycdm/revision/1; *Women's Source Library* (Volume VIII): *Suffrage and the Pankhursts.* Edited by Jane Marcus. London: Routledge, 1987.

31. Packnett, Brittany. "White Celebration vs. Black Riots." *Houston Chronicle*, February 2018. https://m.chron.com/news/media/White-Celebration-vs-Black-Riots-1186829.php; Creighton, Trina T., Curtis L. Walker, and Mark R. Anderson. "Coverage of Black versus White Males in Local Television News Lead Stories." *Journal of Mass Communication Journalism* 4, no. 8 (2014). doi:10.4172/2165-7912.1000216.

32. In "Working through Environmental Despair," Joanna Macy writes: "People are inhibited from expressing their anxieties because they feel that in order to do so they need to be walking data banks and skillful debaters. Taking action on behalf of our common world has unfortunately become confused with winning an argument." Macy, Joanna. "Working through Environmental Despair." In *Ecopsychology: Restoring the Earth, Healing the Mind*, edited by Theodore Roszak, Mary E. Gomes, and Allen D. Kanner, 240–62. San Francisco: Sierra Club Books, 1995.

33. See Fiske, Susan T., Amy J.C. Cuddy, and Peter Glick. "Universal Dimensions of Social Cognition: Warmth and Competence." *Trends in Cognitive Sciences* 11, no. 2 (February 2007): 77–83.

34. Catwright, Samuel. "Diseases and Peculiarities of the Negro Race." *DeBrow's Review*, AMS Press, 1851.

35. Drescher, Jack. "Out of DSM: Depathologizing Homosexuality." *Behavioral Sciences* 5, no. 4 (December 4, 2015): 565–75. https://www.ncbi.nlm.nih.gov/pmc/articles/PMC4695779/. doi:10.3390/bs5040565.

36. See Woodward, Colin Edward. *Marching Masters: Slavery, Race, and the Confederate Army during the Civil War.* Charlottesville: University of Virginia Press, 2014. https://muse.jhu.edu/book/28770.

37. Bargh, John. "The Cognitive Monster: The Case against the Controllability of Automatic Stereotype Effects." In *Dual-Process Theories in Social Psychology*, edited by Shelley Chaiken, 361–82. New York: Guilford Press, 1999; Gerostathos, Antonios, Yvesde Roten, Sylvie Berney, Jean-Nicolas Despland, and Gilles Ambresin. "How Does Addressing Patient's Defenses Help to Repair Alliance Ruptures in Psychodynamic Psychotherapy?" *Journal of Nervous and Mental Disease* 202, no. 5 (2014): 419–24. doi: 10.1097/NMD.00000000 00000112.

38. *Livestock's Long Shadow: Environmental Issues and Options*. Livestock, Environment, and Development Initiative, 2006. http://www.fao.org /docrep/010/a0701e/a0701e.pdf.

Chapter 5

1. "Cassies 2008 Cases: Case Name: New Diamond Shreddies." http:// cassies.ca/content/caselibrary/winners/2009pdfs/REV_C08 _Shreddies.pdf.

2. Our inborn traits, such as our aptitude for introversion or extraversion, also play a role in determining the narratives we construct.

3. See Bush, Julia. "The Anti-Suffrage Movement." *Votes for Women.* British Library, March 5, 2018. https://www.bl.uk/votes-for-women /articles/the-anti-suffrage-movement. See also Jorgensen-Earp, Cheryl R., and Darwin D. Jorgensen. "Physiology and Physical Force: The Effect of Edwardian Science on Women's Suffrage." *Southern Communication Journal* 81, no. 3 (2016): 136–55. doi:10.1080/104 1794X.2015.1124914.

4. Early scholarship on dominant narratives was published by American sociologist W.E.B. Du Bois in his *The Souls of Black Folk* (Chicago: A.C. McClurg & Co., 1903). His references to "the color line," "the veil" and "double-consciousness" describe the operation of a dominant white narrative without using the term explicitly. Developments in sociology and critical theory later in the century saw the conceptual emergence of metanarratives (Jean-Francois Lyotard. *The Postmodern Condition*. Translated by Geoff Bennington and Brian Massumi. Minneapolis: University of Minnesota Press, 1984) and discourses (Michel Foucault. *The Archaeology of Knowledge*. Translated by Alan Sheridan. New York: Pantheon Books, 1972), which argu-

ably laid the theoretical groundwork for the eventual emergence of "dominant narratives." Kimberle Crenshaw's work on intersectionality uses the phrases "dominant ways of thinking," "dominant view," "dominant group control," and "dominant norm," laying further foundations for the current ubiquity of the "dominant (white) narrative." See Crenshaw, Kimberle. "Demarginalizing the Intersection of Race and Sex: A Black Feminist Critique of Antidiscrimination Doctrine, Feminist Theory and Antiracist Politics." *University of Chicago Legal Forum* no. 1 (1989): art. 8. http://chicagounbound.uchicago.edu/uclf/vol1989/iss1/8.

5. Zhao, Yue, Richard Montoro, Karine Igartua, and Brett D. Thombs. "Suicidal Ideation and Attempt among Adolescents Reporting 'Unsure' Sexual Identity or Heterosexual Identity plus Same-Sex Attraction or Behavior: Forgotten Groups." *Journal of the American Academy of Child and Adolescent Psychiatry* 49, no. 2 (2010): 104–13.

6. Haidt, Jonathan. *The Righteous Mind: Why Good People Are Divided by Politics and Religion.* New York: Pantheon Books, 2012.

7. See Applewhite, Ashton. *This Chair Rocks: A Manifesto against Ageism.* New York: Macmillan, 2019.

8. This idea is similar to that of false consciousness, as described by Marxist philosophers; see, for example, Lukács, György. *History and Class Consciousness: Studies in Marxist Dialectics.* Translated by Roger Livingstone. Cambridge: MIT Press, 1971. Originally published in 1923.

9. After the election of American president Barak Obama, the *Wall Street Journal* published an editorial claiming that "[the nation could] put to rest the myth of racism as a barrier to achievement in this splendid country." "President-Elect Obama." *Wall Street Journal*, November 5, 2008, A22. https://www.wsj.com/articles/SB122586244657800863. See Kendi, Ibram X. "The Heartbeat of Racism Is Denial." *New York Times,* January 13, 2018. https://www.nytimes.com/2018/01/13/opinion/sunday/heartbeat-of-racism-denial.html. See also Eddie-Lodge, Reni. *Why I'm No Longer Talking to White People about Race.* London: Bloomsbury, 2018.

10. Sharman, Jon. "'What You're Seeing Isn't Happening,' Trump Tells Veterans' Convention in Meandering Rant against 'Fake News.'" *Independent*, July 25, 2018. https://www.independent.co

.uk/news/world/americas/us-politics/trump-fake-news-veterans
-foreign-wars-video-watch-not-happening-a8462711.html

11. "The Knight/Gallup survey reported that more than 60 percent of the respondents see 'too much bias in the reporting of news stories that are supposed to be objective,' while less than half (44 percent) can identify any news source that they believe reports the news objectively." Knight Foundation. "Why Has Trust in the Government and Media Declined?" *Crisis in Democracy: Renewing Trust in America*. Washington, DC: The Aspen Institute, 2019. See https://kf-site-production.s3.amazonaws.com/media_elements/files/000/000/283/original/Knight_Commission_Report_on_Trust_Media_and_Democracy_FINAL.pdf

12. Nickerson, Raymond. "Confirmation Bias: A Ubiquitous Phenomenon in Many Guises." *Tufts University Review of General Psychology* 2, no. 2 (1998): 175–220.

13. See Coppola, Al. *The Theatre of Experiment: Staging Natural Philosophy in Eighteenth-Century Britain*. Oxford: Oxford University Press, 2016.

14. W.E.B. Du Bois (*The Souls of Black Folk*) and Franz Fanon (*The Wretched of the Earth*. New York: Grove Press, 1963) were the first to write about the deficiency narrative, as it applied to the depiction of black people living under white supremacy.

15. Studies have shown that when we are in positions of power, we are more likely hold others to higher standards than those to which we hold ourselves—we feel justified breaking rules that we expect others to respect. In other words, we feel that we are entitled to what we want, and that others are not. And the opposite is also true: when we are in nonpowerholding positions, we tend to hold ourselves to higher standards than those to which we hold others, and we feel less entitled to break rules and take what we want. See, for example, Robertson, Ian H. "How Power Affects the Brain." *Psychologist* 26 (March 2013): 186–89. https://thepsychologist.bps.org.uk/volume-26/edition-3/how-power-affects-brain.

16. "The World's Women 2015. Work. Chapter 4." United Nations—UN Statistics Division, 2015. https://unstats.un.org/unsd/gender/chapter4/chapter4.html; McHugh, Maureen, and Jennifer Hambaugh. "She

Said, He Said: Gender, Language, and Power." *Handbook of Gender Research in Psychology* 1 (2010): 379–410.

17. Merkel, Wolfgang. "Is Capitalism Compatible with Democracy?" *Comparative Governance and Politics* 8, no. 2 (2014): 109–28; Kornai, Janos. "Centralization and the Capitalist Market Economy." *CESifo Forum* 13, no. 1 (2012): 47–59.

18. See, for example, Keltner, Dacher. *The Power Paradox: How We Gain and Lose Power.* New York: Penguin, 2016. See also Wang, Meifang, and Feng Yang. "The Malleability of Stereotype Effects on Spontaneous Trait Inferences: The Moderating Role of Perceivers' Power." *Social Psychology* 48 (2017): 3–18. https://doi.org/10.1027/1864-9335/a000288.

19. Jean Baker Miller pointed out in *Toward a New Psychology of Women* that to complain is to publicly admit harm, which disrupts the status quo, and that the dominant group tends to suppress complaint through shaming (consider how "complaining" is often feminized and "complainers" are infantilized as "whiners"). Baker Miller, Jean. *Toward a New Psychology of Women.* Boston: Beacon Press, 1987. First published 1976.

20. "Anti-Semitic Incidents Increasing, ADL Says." National Public Radio, October 28, 2018. https://www.npr.org/2018/10/28/661520291/anti-semitic-incidents-increasing-adl-says.

21. Patricia Hill Collins proposed the concept of "controlling images," which are false images—such as that of the "savage" Native American—created by the dominant group about members of the nondominant group that prevent members of the nondominant group from realizing or resisting their oppression. See Collins, Patricia Hill. *Black Feminist Thought: Knowledge, Consciousness, and the Politics of Empowerment.* Boston: Unwin Hyman, 1990.

Chapter 6

1. Crenshaw, Kimberle. "The Urgency of Intersectionality." TEDWomen, October 2016. https://www.ted.com/talks/kimberle_crenshaw_the_urgency_of_intersectionality?language=en.

2. *Intersectionality* is often used inaccurately to describe the ways that oppressions overlap with and reinforce one another. The actual meaning of the term, which Crenshaw intended to be used as a legal definition, is that oppressions which intersect create a new, distinct

category of oppression within which an individual may face a distinct form of discrimination. For example, a black woman is not merely "doubly" oppressed but faces a whole separate type of discrimination than does a white woman or a black man.

3. The concept of privilege is believed to have been first published in 1903 by W.E.B. Du Bois in his essay *The Souls of Black Folk*, and it was later popularized through Peggy McIntosh's 1988 essay "White Privilege and Male Privilege: A Personal Account of Coming to See Correspondences through Work in Women's Studies." Working paper 189. Wellesley, MA: Center for Research on Women, 1988. Available online at https://nationalseedproject.org/Key-SEED-Texts/white-privilege-and-male-privilege.

4. Sherer, Mark, James E. Maddux, Blaise Mercandante, Steven Prentice-Dunn, Beth Jacobs, and Ronald W. Rogers. "The Self-Efficacy Scale: Construction and Validation." *Psychological Reports* 51, no. 2 (1982): 663–71.

5. McNamee, Stephen J., and Robert B. Miller Jr. *The Meritocracy Myth*. Lanham, MD: Rowman & Littlefield, 2004.

6. Nagahawatte, Tanya N., and Robert L. Goldenberg. "Poverty, Maternal Health, and Adverse Pregnancy Outcomes." *Annals of the New York Academy of Sciences* 1136 (2008): 80–85.

7. Clark, Kenneth B., and Mamie P. Clark. "Emotional Factors in Racial Identification and Preference in Negro Children." *The Journal of Negro Education* 19, no. 3 (Summer, 1950): 341–350. http://www.jstor.org/stable/2966491; Jordan, Phillip, and Maria Hernandez-Reif. "Reexamination of Young Children's Racial Attitudes and Skin Tone Preferences." *Journal of Black Psychology* 35, no. 3 (2009): 388–403.

8. If, however, the person crossing our boundary has more social power than we have and especially if we perceive that power as deserved—if they are someone famous, for example—we may be less likely to notice or be offended by the violation.

9. Johnson, Allan G. *Privilege, Power, and Difference*. New York: McGraw-Hill Education, 2005.

10. Ferguson, Sian. "Privilege 101: A Quick and Dirty Guide," September 29, 2014, p. 5. https://theavarnagroup.com/wp-content/uploads/2016/01/Privilege-101.pdf.

11. See, for example, DiAngelo, Robin. *White Fragility: Why It's So Hard for White People to Talk about Racism.* Boston: Beacon Press, 2018.

12. Hänsel, Alexander, and Roland von Känel. "The Ventro-Medial Prefrontal Cortex: A Major Link between the Autonomic Nervous System, Regulation of Emotion, and Stress Reactivity?" *BioPsychoSocial Medicine* 2, no. 21 (2008). https://doi.org/10.1186/1751-0759-2 -21. See also Mobbs, Dean, Predrag Petrovic, Jennifer L. Marchant, Demis Hassabis, Nikolaus Weiskopf, Ben Seymour, Raymond J. Dolan, and Christopher D. Frith. "When Fear Is Near: Threat Imminence Elicits Prefrontal-Periaqueductal Gray Shifts in Humans." *Science*, August 24, 2007, 1079–83.

13. Dr. A. Breeze Harper's experiences as a vegan activist are telling: "I have faced opposition really only from post-racial white middle class vegans who are 'single issue' and are so invested in their racial-class privilege (at the unconscious level in many cases) that they simply cannot admit that white privilege, race and class still matter in the USA." See Petersson-Martin, Kira. "#TBT: An interview with Dr. A. Breeze Harper." *T.O.F.U. Magazine*, May 2016. ilovetofu. ca/2016/05/05/tbt-an-interview-with-dr-a-breeze-harper/.

14. See Larson, Stephanie Greco. *Media and Minorities: The Politics of Race in News and Entertainment.* New York: Rowman & Littlefield, 2006.

15. Duarte, José L., Jarret T. Crawford, Charlotta Stern, Jonathan Haidt, Lee J. Philip, and Philip E. Tetlock. "Political Diversity Will Improve Social Psychology Science." *Behavioural and Brain Sciences* 38 (2015), E130. https://doi.org/10.1017/S0140525X1400043.

16. Of course, it's also important for us to be privilege literate when we're in a disadvantaged position, but a just redistribution of power requires that more of the burden of transformation be carried by those who have benefited from a powerarchy.

17. Emotional labor is the uncompensated work of managing essential yet often invisible tasks involving emotion.

Chapter 7

1. Linda Hartling and Elizabeth Sparks described systems that are not power over as "cultures of connection," suggesting they are organized

around "growth through relationship, mutual empowerment, responsiveness, authenticity, and movement toward mutuality." Hartling, Linda, and Elizabeth Sparks. "Relational Cultural Practice: Working in a Nonrelational World." In *The Power of Connection: Recent Developments in Relational-Cultural Theory*, edited by Judith V. Jordan, 162. New York: Routledge, 2010.

2. It is interesting to note that, of the five moral values that inform one's political orientation, compassion and justice—the two values that underlie progressive politics—may be the most likely to balance power. The other three values are loyalty/in-group standing, authority/respect, and purity/sanctity. For more information on moral values and political orientations, see MoralFoundations.Org, https://www.moralfoundations.org, and YourMorals.Org, https://www.yourmorals.org/.

3. Although feminism emerged as a countersystem to the powerarchy of patriarchy, feminism has not been without problems. As with all systems, including countersystems, feminism must continue to examine its own assumptions and grow in integrity. For example, traditional feminism has rightly been criticized for being a movement of and for white women.

4. Nhat Hanh, Thich. *Interbeing*. New Delhi: Full Circle, 2009.

5. "I have a dream that one day this nation will rise up and live out the true meaning of its creed: 'We hold these truths to be self-evident, that all men are created equal.'" King, Martin L., Jr. "I Have a Dream." Speech at the Lincoln Memorial, Washington, DC, August 28, 1963. Available at American Rhetoric. https://www.americanrhetoric.com/speeches/mlkihaveadream.htm.

6. These are not to be confused with Hartling and Sparks's "pseudo-relational cultures," which are systems with conflict-averse participants who avoid authenticity in order to keep the peace. Hartling and Sparks, "Relational Cultural Practice." In *Power of Connection*, edited by Jordan, 158–81.

7. Note that here I am referring to all types of fundamentalist systems, not simply religious ones.

8. An excellent book on preventing and treating this kind of traumatic stress is van Dernoot Lipsky, Laura, and Connie Burk. *Trauma Stewardship*. Oakland, CA: Berrett-Koehler, 2009.

9. Coddington, Kate. "Contagious Trauma: Reframing the Spatial Mobility of Trauma within Advocacy Work." *Emotion, Space and Society* 24 (August 2017): 66–73.

10. For an informative discussion on resilience and relationality, see Hartling, Linda M. "Strengthening Resilience in a Risky World: It's All about Relationships." In *Power of Connection*, edited by Jordan, 49–68.

11. As mentioned in chapter 5, examining the potential impact of traumatization on advocates of countersystems is not meant to pathologize them or discredit their actions. It is simply meant to point out that power-over dynamics can and often do end up being re-created when there is a lack of awareness of the process of power, and particularly when certain aggravating factors, such as traumatization, are present.

12. Wilkins, Clara L., and Cheryl R. Kaiser. "Racial Progress as Threat to the Status Hierarchy: Implications for Perceptions of Anti-White Bias." *Psychological Science* 25, no. 2 (February 2014): 439–46. doi: 10.1177/0956797613508412.

13. The rise of the men's rights movement since the 1970s, which was sparked as a "counterrevolution" to the second wave of feminism, is a clear example of this. Notable groups are Men's Rights Incorporated, the National Coalition for Men, and the National Organization of Men.

14. Hicks, Donna. *Dignity: The Essential Role It Plays in Resolving Conflict.* New Haven, CT: Yale University Press, 2011.

15. Hicks, *Dignity.*

16. Goleman, Daniel. *Emotional Intelligence: Why It Can Matter More Than IQ.* New York: Bantam, 1995.

17. See Lakin, Jessica L., Valerie E. Jefferis, Clara Michelle Cheng, and Tanya L. Chartrand. "The Chameleon Effect as Social Glue: Evidence for the Evolutionary Significance of Nonconscious Mimicry." *Journal of Nonverbal Behavior* 27 (2003): 145–62. https://doi.org/10.1023/A:1025389814290. See also Chartrand, Tanya L., and John A. Bargh. "The Chameleon Effect: The Perception-Behavior Link and Social Interaction." *Journal of Personality and Social Psychology* 76 (1999): 893–910.

18. Zenger, Jack, and Joseph Folkman. "The Ideal Praise-to-Criticism Ratio." *Harvard Business Review*, March 15, 2013. https://hbr.org/2013/03/the-ideal-praise-to-criticism.

19. Tugend, Alina. "Praise Is Fleeting, but Brickbats We Recall." *New York Times*, March 23, 2012. https://www.nytimes.com/2012/03/24/your -money/why-people-remember-negative-events-more-than-positive -ones.html.

20. Foulk, Trevor, Andrew Woolum, and Amir Erez. "Catching Rudeness Is Like Catching a Cold: The Contagion Effects of Low-Intensity Negative Behaviors." *Journal of Applied Psychology* 101, no. 1 (June 29, 2015): 50–67. doi: 10.1037/apl0000037.

21. This notion is similar to Eckhart Tolle's description of the ego. See Tolle, Eckhart. *The Power of Now: A Guide to Spiritual Enlightenment.* Novato, CA: New World Library, 1999.

22. See "Trauma as a Precursor to Violent Extremism." START, April 2015. https://www.start.umd.edu/pubs/START_CSTAB_Trau maAsPrecursortoViolentExtremism_April2015.pdf.

23. See Picciolini, Christian. *Romantic Violence: Memoirs of an American Skinhead.* Chicago: Goldmill Group, 2015.

24. See, for example, *The Power Paradox* by Dacher Keltner.

25. Lerner, Harriet. *The Dance of Connection.* New York: William Morrow Paperbacks, 2002.

26. Goleman, *Emotional Intelligence.*

27. See McKay, Matthew, Martha Davis, and Patrick Fanning. *Messages: The Communication Skills Book.* Oakland, CA: New Harbinger, 2009; and Paterson, Randy J. *The Assertiveness Workbook: How to Express Your Ideas and Stand Up for Yourself at Work and in Relationships* (A New Harbinger Self-Help Workbook). Oakland, CA: New Harbinger, 2000.

28. Fletcher, Clive, and Caroline Bailey. "Assessing Self-Awareness: Some Issues and Methods." *Journal of Managerial Psychology* 18, no. 5 (2003): 395–404. https://doi.org/10.1108/02683940310484008.

29. Vago, David R., and David A. Silbersweig. "Self-Awareness, Self-Regulation, and Self-Transcendence (S-ART): A Framework for Understanding the Neurobiological Mechanisms of Mindfulness." *Frontiers of Human Neuroscience*, October 25, 2012. www.ncbi.nlm .nih.gov/pubmed/23112770.

30. Tang, Yi-Yuan, Qilin Lu, Xiujuan Geng, Elliot A. Stein, Yihong Yang, and Michael I. Posner. "Short-Term Meditation Induces White Matter Changes in the Anterior Cingulate." *PNAS* 107,

no. 35 (August 31, 2010): 15649–52. https://doi.org/10.1073/pnas .1011043107.

31. Learning Cognitive-Behavioral Therapy (CBT) is an excellent way to develop the inner observer.

32. Tod, David, James Hardy, and Emily Oliver. "Effects of Self-Talk: A Systematic Review." *Journal of Sport & Exercise Psychology* 33 (2011): 666–87. doi:10.1123/jsep.33.5.666.

33. Nonviolent communication was developed by Marshall Rosenberg (see Rosenberg, Marshall B. *Nonviolent Communication: A Language of Life.* Encinitas, CA: Puddeldancer Press, 2015). I recommend a slightly modified version of the original method, as put forth in *Messages* by McKay, Davis, and Fanning.

34. There is evidence of a natural progression from competitive toward cooperative game-playing strategies when the latter are sufficiently rewarded, and the rewarding is itself a form of cooperation. See Tampuu, Ardi, Tambet Matiisen, Dorian Kodelja, Ilya Kuzovkin, Kristjan Korjus, Juhan Aru, Jaan Aru, and Raul Vicente. "Multiagent Cooperation and Competition with Deep Reinforcement Learning." *PLoS ONE* 12, no. 4 (April 5, 2017): e0172395. https:// doi.org/10.1371/journal.pone.0172395.

Chapter 8

1. Ko, Aph, and Syl Ko. *Aphro-ism: Essays on Pop Culture, Feminism, and Black Veganism from Two Sisters.* New York: Lantern Books, 2017. Also see Lorde, Audre. "The Great American Disease." *Black Scholar* 10, no. 8/9 (1979): 17–20.

2. For excellent resources on privilege, see David, E.J.R., and Annie O. Derthick. *The Psychology of Oppression.* New York: Springer, 2017; Johnson, Allan G. *Privilege, Power, and Difference.* New York: McGraw-Hill Education, 2005.

3. "The Facts behind the #metoo Movement: A National Study on Sexual Harassment and Assault." Stop Street Harassment, February 2018. http://www.stopstreetharassment.org/wp-content/uploads /2018/01/Full-Report-2018-National-Study-on-Sexual-Harassment -and-Assault.pdf; "Victims of Sexual Violence: Statistics" RAINN, 2018. https://www.rainn.org/statistics/victims-sexual-violence.

4. Herman, Judith. *Trauma and Recovery: The Aftermath of Violence—From Domestic Abuse to Political Terror.* New York: Basic Books, 2015. First published 1992. See also Courtois, Christine A. "Complex Trauma, Complex Reactions: Assessment and Treatment." *Psychological Trauma: Theory, Research, Practice, and Policy* S, no. 1 (2008): 86–100. http://dx.doi.org/10.1037/1942-9681.S.1.86.

5. Weingarten, Kaethe. *Common Shock: Witnessing Violence Every Day—How We Are Harmed, How We Can Heal.* New York: Dutton, 2003.

6. See "Press Releases: Facing the Truth." BBC, September 24, 2014. http://www.bbc.co.uk/pressoffice/pressreleases/stories/2006/02_february/14/truth.shtml.

7. See works by Terrence Real—for example, *Terry Real: New Rules for Couples.* Relational Life Institute, 2017. http://www.terryreal.com/.

8. Describing the rigidity and porousness of psychological boundaries is not meant to oversimplify this complex issue but to point out a key way that boundaries can be affected by privilege and oppression. It is also worth noting that one of the central features of trauma is its impact on psychological boundaries; trauma involves boundary violations, often by once-trusted individuals, and it can cause survivors to struggle to develop secure psychological boundaries. Likewise, those who are targets of oppression may have a similar struggle.

9. I am referring here to the treatment of those about whom the person or people calling out have little information. I am not referring to deeply problematic, oppressive powerholding individuals and institutions, such as Donald Trump and his administration, whose motivations are well documented and corroborated.

10. The notion of calling out originated in black social justice circles as an important way to challenge racism by naming oppressive behaviors and policies and holding the offending individuals and institutions accountable. However, the practice of calling out has become mainstreamed, and it is not always used toward its original ends.

11. See, for example, Erskine, Richard G. "Shame and Self-Righteousness: Transactional Analysis Perspectives and Clinical Interventions." *Transactional Analysis Journal* 24, no. 2 (1994): 86–102.

12. See Trần, N. Loan. "Calling IN: A Less Disposable Way of Holding Each Other Accountable." Humanity in Action, December 2013. https://www.humanityinaction.org/files/567-N.Trn-CallingIN.pdf.

13. Adams, Carol J. *Neither Man nor Beast: Feminism and the Defense of Animals*. New York: Lantern Books, 2015.
14. Lieberman, Matthew D. *Hardwired for Connection: Why Our Brains Are Wired to Connect*. New York: Broadway Books, 2014. See also Banks, Amy, and Leigh Ann Hirschman. *Wired to Connect: The Surprising Link between Brain Science and Strong, Healthy Relationships*. New York: TarcherPerigee, 2016.
15. Tutu, Desmond, "Made for Goodness." (Jan. 12, 2012). Available at: https://www.huffpost.com/entry/made-for-goodness_b_1199864.

GLOSSARY

abuse
the unjust allocation and use of power; can be a single behavior or systemic (in a dyadic relationship or in a group dynamic)

authoritarianism
the belief that power should be concentrated in the hands of those deemed appropriate to exercise authority over others and that such authority is more valuable than individual freedoms

awareness
a state of mindful observation; (on a practical level, as with social issues) a state of intellectual and emotional understanding

backlash
the reaction of a social powerarchy to its power being threatened in an attempt to regain lost power

carnism
the ideology that conditions people to eat the flesh and other products of certain animals

closed system
a system that is closed to change (and on which powerarchy is based)

cognitive dissonance
the psychological discomfort that arises when our values or beliefs and behaviors are contradictory

cognitive distortions
one of the three defenses of powerarchies, a set of myths that distort our perceptions and numb our feelings so that we support the powerarchy; each distortion acts as a distancing mechanism that disconnects us from our rationality, empathy, and, ultimately, integrity

compassionate witnessing
paying attention and listening with empathy and compassion and without judgment (a term coined by psychologist Kaethe Weingarten)

confirmation bias
the tendency for people to seek, notice, and remember only information that supports their existing assumptions, that confirms their narrative

counternarrative
a narrative that challenges a dominant narrative; often, a narrative of a countersystem

countersystem
a system designed to counter a powerarchy (e.g., feminism or veganism)

defining reality
dictating the truth of another's experience—appointing oneself the expert on what another is thinking or feeling, even when they say otherwise

deindividualization
perceiving someone as an abstraction, as lacking individuality or a personality; a cognitive distortion

dichotomization
placing individuals into oppositional categories in our minds so that we harbor different feelings and carry out different behaviors toward members of different groups; a cognitive distortion

dignity
one's sense of inherent worth

disempowered
lacking or feeling that one lacks the ability to act or influence; a person can be disempowered (lacking agency), or they can feel disempowered (lacking belief in agency that they actually have).

disempowerment
the state of lacking the ability to act or influence, or of lacking the belief that we have the ability to act or influence (which often includes a diminished sense of self-worth)

dominant narrative
the narrative of the individual or group with more power in a powerarchy

empowered
having the ability to act or influence or the feeling someone has when they possess such an ability (For an elaboration on this definition, see note 5 from chapter 2.)

empowerment
the state of having the ability to act or influence or of the belief that we have the ability to act or influence—even if what we can act on or influence is simply how we mentally or emotionally respond to events; this state often includes the sense of being worthy

entitlement
believing that we are deserving of special treatment, that the rules we expect others to follow don't apply to us

grandiosity
the flip side of shame; the feeling or sense of being superior, or more worthy than others

healthy relational behaviors
behaviors that create a sense of connection and foster a sense of security and mutual empowerment and that reflect integrity and honor dignity

hierarchy of moral worth (belief in)
the belief that some individuals or groups are more worthy of moral consideration—of being treated with integrity—than others

humility
the opposite of grandiosity; the recognition that we are not more worthy than others; the feeling or sense of being as worthy as others

institutionalized powerarchy
powerarchy that is embraced and maintained by social institutions

integrity
the integration of core moral values, most notably compassion and justice, and behaviors

internalized oppression
the phenomenon whereby those with less power in a powerarchy believe in their inferiority and often act in ways that mirror and reinforce this belief

internalized powerarchy
believing the myths of powerarchy such that one feels either morally superior or inferior to others, and often acting accordingly

internalized privilege
the flip side of internalized oppression; the phenomenon whereby dominant individuals or groups in a powerarchy believe in their superiority and thus feel entitled to special treatment that is withheld from others, and they act accordingly

mindfulness
a strategy, or practice, and a state; it is at once a tool for developing awareness and also a state of presence, of being present in the moment

myths
fictitious stories of a powerarchy that help maintain the system

narrative
a story that's created based on beliefs and perceptions; powerarchy narratives are stories that reflect cognitive distortions and that weave such stories together to create an even stronger defensive structure; along with cognitive distortions and privileges, one of the three defenses of powerarchies

nonrelational behaviors
behaviors that create a sense of disconnection, foster a sense of insecurity and disempowerment, and violate integrity and harm dignity

objectification
perceiving someone as an object; a cognitive distortion

open system
a system that is open to change

oppression
the unjust allocation and use—the abuse—of power, on systemic, institutional levels

othering
seeing others as fundamentally different from and inferior to oneself

physical disempowerment
lacking the ability to act or influence

power
the capacity or ability to influence others, oneself, or events to bring about a desired outcome

power dynamic
an interaction (two or more behaviors) that reflects and reinforces a power model (e.g., a power-with dynamic)

power literacy
understanding the nature and structure of power dynamics, including how having (or not having) power impacts thoughts, feelings, and behaviors

power model
a framework or guide for how and why to use our power, including how to increase our sense of power; it informs our process and dynamics, and it also informs, and is informed by, a type of system (a powerarchy or a power-with system)

power-over behavior
a behavior that reflects and reinforces the power-over model

power-over model (also referred to as the dominance model or the competitive power model)
the model of power in which we place our interests over those of others or of the relationship of which we are a part; we use our power to get what we want, to serve our own ends, without regard for the interests of others. This model informs, and is informed by, powerarchy.

power role
a role based on an unequal distribution of power

power-with behavior

a behavior that reflects and reinforces a the power-with model

power-with/functionalist model (also referred to as the cooperative power model)

the model of power in which we place our interests alongside the interests of others and of the relationship or group as a whole

power-with system (also referred to as a system of integrity)

the opposite of powerarchy; a relational system that is organized around the belief that all individuals are of equal moral worth and that is structured to prevent unjust power imbalances

powerarchy

a nonrelational system that is organized around the belief in a hierarchy of moral worth and that is structured to maintain an unjust power imbalance

powerful

having, or believing one has, the ability to act or influence; can also refer to the feeling that accompanies such a state or belief

powerholder

the individual or group with more power in a system (the imbalance of power in the system is not always unjust, as with a family system whereby the parent is the powerholder)

practical privilege

a practical advantage that is unfairly denied to others

presence

the state of being in the present moment; also referred to as being in a state of mindfulness

pride
the opposite of shame; the recognition that we are not less worthy than others; the feeling or sense of being as worthy as others

primary cognitive distortions
distortions that validate powerarchy or a particular powerarchy

privilege
an advantage that is unfairly denied to others; along with cognitive distortions and narratives, one of the three defenses of powerarchies

privilege literacy
knowing the facts about privilege (about the oppression the privilege defends and about the structure of the privilege itself), as well as understanding the meaning of those facts; awareness, which is both an intellectual and emotional state. When we are privilege literate, we are informed about the nature and structure of our privilege, and we empathize with those who are impacted by it.

process of power
the method we use that informs our power dynamics; the process includes behaviors but is broader than behaviors, as it includes our agenda or intentions as well

projection
projecting onto proponents of a countersystem negative and inaccurate ideas about them that invalidate their message (when used as a secondary cognitive distortion)

pseudo power-with system
a powerarchy that appears to be a power-with system

psychological disempowerment
lacking the belief in one's ability to act or influence (which often, though not always, includes a diminished sense of self-worth)

psychological privilege
the result of the myths that obscure and justify privilege being turned into narratives that teach us to buy into the very assumptions and attitudes that help structures of privilege remain unchallenged

relational dimensions
the levels on which we engage in relational dynamics, which include the intrapersonal (within the individual, as when we are relating to ourselves), the interpersonal (between two or more individuals), and the collective (between or among social groups); these dimensions also include our relationships with nonhuman beings and the environment

relational literacy
the ability to understand and express healthy ways of relating, which includes emotional intelligence, self-awareness, mindfulness, and effective communication skills

resilient
being able to withstand and bounce back from stress

role
the part we play in a system, such as "father," "colleague," or "advocate"

rule
the guideline that dictates how individuals should behave and experience themselves (and others) in their roles

secondary cognitive distortions
distortions that invalidate the countersystem that challenges a powerarchy

self-awareness
the capacity to reflect on our thoughts, feelings, personality, identity, resources, and other aspects of our personal and internal experiences

shame
the feeling or sense of being inferior, or less worthy than others

social powerarchy
a powerarchy that exists on the social level, such as racism or sexism (and that informs interpersonal powerarchies that reflect the same kinds of power dynamics)

social powerarchy narratives
the dominant narratives that mirror and bolster the mythology of a social powerarchy and that members of all groups—dominant and nondominant—grow up learning and believing

system
a set of interconnected parts that form a whole

trauma narrative
a worldview that is based on trauma, whereby we see the world as one ongoing traumatic event with only three roles to be played: victim, perpetrator, and hero

ACKNOWLEDGMENTS

I am deeply grateful for the support of the many people who made writing this book possible. I thank my team of compassionate and hardworking change agents for providing me with a foundation for my work, for their ongoing encouragement, and—along with the ProVeg team—for making the world a more just and compassionate place: Craig Brierly, Tobias Leenaert, Ceri Flook, and Johan Peter Sundberg, these thanks go to you—and thanks especially to Flavia D'Erasmo and Christina Galego, who worked tirelessly to support this project. I am incredibly grateful for my agent, Marilyn Allen, who believed in this project and worked to make sure it found the perfect home; and for Gero Schomaker for helping me hone my ideas and reconceptualize concepts and also for being a great person and a good friend. I am so grateful for my amazing editor, Anna Leinberger, for her wisdom, encouragement, and championing of this project, and all the fabulous people at Berrett-Koehler, with whom it has been my honor to work. I thank Jim Greenbaum, without whose support this book would probably never have been written and also Meghan Lowery, whose support and friendship have helped me along the way. I also thank Ari Nessel for being a part of the foundational support that keeps me inspired and able to focus on the work I need to do. I thank Joyce Hildebrand for helping shape this book during its inception, and Marc Bekoff, for supporting me in the submissions process and for his important contributions to helping create a more compassionate world. I thank Christopher-Sebastian McJetters for his guidance and critical insights, and also for his wonderful friendship. I am grateful for my dear friends Susan Solomon and Kathy Freston for all their support and encouragement of me as a person and as a writer over the years we've known each other. I am so grateful for my colleague and dear friend Dawn Moncrief, whose support is infused throughout all my projects and who went above and beyond for this one. I am grateful for the invaluable insights provided by Leah Nunke and for the creative support provided by Roxy Vélez, and I thank the many people who took the time to review earlier drafts and give me feedback on them; in particular, I am grateful to Jens Tuider, Aryenish Birdie, Carolyn Zaikowski, Liz Ross, Melanie Gold, Chantal Prinsloo, Victoria Yates, Wilke Seekles, Elliot Gold, Bonnie Gramlich, Vique Mora, Alexandra Navarro, Silvania Pezzetta, Beatrice Frasl, Julia Aumüller, Diane Coetzer, Orit Kamir, Paul Gorski, and Leah Edgerton. Finally, this book would not have been possible without the support of Sebastian Joy, my husband, muse, and partner in working to cultivate a more relational world.

INDEX

Endnotes are referred to by page number and note number (*n* or *nn*).

ABOUT THE AUTHOR

MELANIE JOY, PHD, EDM, is a Harvard-educated psychologist, international speaker, and organizational and relationship coach. She is the author of three other books, including the award-winning *Why We Love Dogs, Eat Pigs, and Wear Cows: An Introduction to Carnism.* Dr. Joy was a lecturer at the University of Massachusetts, Boston, for 11 years, where she taught courses on privilege and oppression, feminist psychology, and animal rights. She has given talks and trainings on six continents and in over 45 countries, and her work has been featured in major media outlets around the world. She is the eighth recipient of the Ahimsa Award—previously given to the Dalai Lama and Nelson Mandela—for her work on global nonviolence. Dr. Joy is also the founding president of the charitable organization Beyond Carnism. You can learn more about her work at powerarchy.org.

Berrett–Koehler
Publishers

Berrett-Koehler is an independent publisher dedicated to an ambitious mission: *Connecting people and ideas to create a world that works for all.*

Our publications span many formats, including print, digital, audio, and video. We also offer online resources, training, and gatherings. And we will continue expanding our products and services to advance our mission.

We believe that the solutions to the world's problems will come from all of us, working at all levels: in our society, in our organizations, and in our own lives. Our publications and resources offer pathways to creating a more just, equitable, and sustainable society. They help people make their organizations more humane, democratic, diverse, and effective (and we don't think there's any contradiction there). And they guide people in creating positive change in their own lives and aligning their personal practices with their aspirations for a better world.

And we strive to practice what we preach through what we call "The BK Way." At the core of this approach is *stewardship,* a deep sense of responsibility to administer the company for the benefit of all of our stakeholder groups, including authors, customers, employees, investors, service providers, sales partners, and the communities and environment around us. Everything we do is built around stewardship and our other core values of *quality, partnership, inclusion,* and *sustainability.*

This is why Berrett-Koehler is the first book publishing company to be both a B Corporation (a rigorous certification) and a benefit corporation (a for-profit legal status), which together require us to adhere to the highest standards for corporate, social, and environmental performance. And it is why we have instituted many pioneering practices (which you can learn about at www.bkconnection.com), including the Berrett-Koehler Constitution, the Bill of Rights and Responsibilities for BK Authors, and our unique Author Days.

We are grateful to our readers, authors, and other friends who are supporting our mission. We ask you to share with us examples of how BK publications and resources are making a difference in your lives, organizations, and communities at www.bkconnection.com/impact.

Dear reader,

Thank you for picking up this book and welcome to the worldwide BK community! You're joining a special group of people who have come together to create positive change in their lives, organizations, and communities.

What's BK all about?

Our mission is to connect people and ideas to create a world that works for all.

Why? Our communities, organizations, and lives get bogged down by old paradigms of self-interest, exclusion, hierarchy, and privilege. But we believe that can change. That's why we seek the leading experts on these challenges—and share their actionable ideas with you.

A welcome gift

To help you get started, we'd like to offer you a **free copy** of one of our bestselling ebooks:

www.bkconnection.com/welcome

When you claim your **free ebook**, you'll also be subscribed to our blog.

Our freshest insights

Access the best new tools and ideas for leaders at all levels on our blog at ideas.bkconnection.com.

Sincerely,

Your friends at Berrett-Koehler

Certified

Corporation